Praise for

the HONEYMOON EFFECT

"A truly remarkable achievement . . . a lifetime of joy all delivered in one concise manuscript. I've read it twice, and I loved every minute I spent with it. One of my favorite reads ever."

—Dr. Wayne W. Dyer

"Bruce Lipton has written the single best book on love—both personal and planetary—that I've ever read. And I've read a lot of them! I know Bruce and his beloved Margaret up close and personal. Their relationship is joyful, nurturing, creative, and contagious. They live in Heaven on Earth and so can you. Bruce uses the principles of the New Science he champions to enlighten, explain, and encourage us all to embody the love that we've always wanted."

—Joan Borysenko, Ph.D.,
biologist, psychologist, and best-selling author of *Minding the Body, Mending the Mind*

"If you've ever wondered why an exciting, new relationship loses its magic and shine, you'll want to read this book. By understanding the science behind how we relate to others, and learning the strategies to successfully connect in the best possible way, **The Honeymoon Effect** *is sure to bring the luster and life back to the relationships that matter most."*

—Cheryl Richardson, author of *You Can Create an Exceptional Life, The Art of Extreme Self-Care, The Unmistakable Touch of Grace, Stand Up for Your Life, Life Makeovers,* and *Take Time for Your Life*

"What a pleasure to read Bruce's entertaining romp through the science of loving relationships! Bruce makes it clear that couples can learn a lot from the quantum physics, biochemistry, and psychology that promote conscious, loving relationships. Great reading for anyone who wants to bring a loving relationship into his or her life—or maintain one that already exists."

—Gay Hendricks, Ph.D., author of *The Big Leap* and (with Dr. Kathlyn Hendricks) *Conscious Loving*

"The Honeymoon Effect *is a must-read for every couple striving to create love and trust in their relationship. Bruce's readable explanation of the science behind the magic of love is engaging, inspiring, and, most of all, enlightening!"*

—Arielle Ford, author of *Wabi Sabi Love*

"A brilliant and cohesive explanation of how we fall in love—and how we lose it once the Honeymoon Effect passes. Happily, Lipton gives us an equally clear explanation of how we can modify our subconscious programming and transform our most fundamental patterns in order to reclaim the Honeymoon Effect in all our relationships for the rest of our lives. Lipton draws on cell biology, the study of noble gases, and conscious parenting (among other things) to make his points, yet brings a lighthearted simplicity that is both joyful and profound in its implications. As with all of Lipton's work, this book delivers!"

—Nicki Scully, author of *Alchemical Healing* and *Planetary Healing*

the HONEYMOON EFFECT

ALSO BY BRUCE H. LIPTON, PH.D.

Books

*The Biology of Belief: Unleashing the Power of Consciousness, Matter & Miracles**

*Spontaneous Evolution: Our Positive Future (and a Way to Get There from Here)**

CDs/DVDs

The Biology of Belief: Unleashing the Power of Consciousness, Matter & Miracles

*An Introduction to Spontaneous Evolution**

Spontaneous Evolution: Our Positive Future and How to Get There from Here

The Wisdom of Your Cells: How Your Beliefs Control Your Biology

*Available from Hay House
Please visit:

Hay House USA: **www.hayhouse.com®**
Hay House Australia: **www.hayhouse.com.au**
Hay House UK: **www.hayhouse.co.uk**
Hay House India: **www.hayhouse.co.in**

the HONEYMOON EFFECT

the science of creating heaven on earth

Bruce H. Lipton, Ph.D.

HAY HOUSE, INC.
Carlsbad, California • New York City
London • Sydney • New Delhi

Published in the United States by: Hay House LLC: www.hayhouse.com®
Published in Australia by: Hay House Australia Pty. Ltd.: www.hayhouse.com.au
Published in the United Kingdom by: Hay House UK, Ltd.: www.hayhouse.co.uk
Published in India by: Hay House Publishers India: www.hayhouse.co.in

Indexer: Susan Edwards • *Cover design:* Robert Mueller • *Interior design:* Pamela Homan • *Page 49 illustration:* Robert Mueller

The author of this book does not dispense medical advice or prescribe the use of any technique as a form of treatment for physical, emotional, or medical problems without the advice of a physician, either directly or indirectly. The intent of the author is only to offer information of a general nature to help you in your quest for emotional and spiritual well-being. In the event you use any of the information in this book for yourself, the author and the publisher assume no responsibility for your actions.

Library of Congress Cataloging-in-Publication Data

Lipton, Bruce H.
The honeymoon effect : the science of creating heaven on earth / Bruce H. Lipton, Ph.D. -- 1st edition.
pages cm
Includes bibliographical references and index.
ISBN 978-1-4019-2386-0 (hardcover : alk. paper) 1. Man-woman relationships. 2. Interpersonal relationships. I. Title.
HQ801.L4935 2013
302--dc23

2012048478

ISBN: 978-1-4019-2389-1

24 23 22 21 20 19 18 17 16 15
1st edition, May 2013

Printed in the United States of America

This product uses responsibly sourced papers and/or recycled materials. For more information, see www.hayhouse.com.

For
Heaven on Earth
Through
Love for ourselves
Love for one another
Love for our planet

CONTENTS

The Honeymoon Effect:
A state of bliss, passion, energy, and health resulting from a huge love. Your life is so beautiful that you can't wait to get up to start a new day and thank the Universe that you are alive.

INTRODUCTION

A lifetime without Love is of no account
Love is the Water of Life
Drink it down with heart and soul

—Rumi

When I was young, if anyone had ever told me I would be writing a book about relationships, I'd have told them they were out of their mind. I thought love was a myth dreamed up by poets and Hollywood producers to make people feel bad about what they could never have. Everlasting love? Happily Ever After? Forget about it.

Like everyone, I was programmed in a way that enabled some things in my life to come naturally. My programming emphasized the importance of education. To my parents, the value of an education was the difference between the life of a ditchdigger just getting by and a white-collar executive with soft hands and a soft life. They were clearly of the opinion that "You cannot amount to anything in this world without an education."

Given their beliefs, unsurprisingly, my parents held nothing back when it came to expanding my educational horizons. I vividly recall coming home from Mrs. Novak's second-grade class thrilled by my first look into the amazing microscopic world of single-celled amoebas and beautiful unicellular algae like the fascinatingly named spirogyra. I burst into the house and begged my mother for a microscope of my own. Without any hesitation, she immediately drove me to the store and bought me my first microscope. This was clearly not the same response to the tantrum I had thrown over my desperate desire to get a Roy Rogers cowboy hat, six-shooter, and holster!

Despite my Roy Rogers phase, it was Albert Einstein who became the iconic hero of my youth: my Mickey Mantle, Cary Grant, and Elvis Presley all rolled into one giant personality. I always loved the photo that showed him sticking out his tongue, his head covered with an exploding shock of white hair. I also loved seeing Einstein on the tiny screen of the (newly invented) television in our living room where he appeared as a loving, wise, and playful grandparent.

Most of all, I took great pride in the fact that Einstein, a Jewish immigrant like my father, overcame prejudice through his scientific brilliance. At times while growing up in Westchester County, New York, I felt like an outcast; there were parents in our town who refused to allow me to play with their kids lest I spread "Bolshevism" to them. It gave me a feeling of pride and security to know that Einstein, far from being an outcast, was a Jewish man who was respected and honored around the world.

Good teachers, my education-is-all family, and my passion for spending hours at my microscope led to a Ph.D. in cell biology and a tenured position at the University of Wisconsin School of Medicine and Public Health. Ironically, it was only when I left my position there to explore the "new science," including studies on quantum mechanics, that I began to understand the profound nature of my boyhood hero Einstein's contributions to our world.

While I flourished academically, in other areas I was a poster child for dysfunction, especially in the realm of relationships. I married in my 20s when I was too young and too emotionally immature to be ready for a meaningful relationship. When after ten years of marriage I told my father I was getting divorced, he adamantly argued against it and told me, "Marriage is a business."

In hindsight, my father's response made sense for someone who emigrated in 1919 from a Russia engulfed in famine, pogroms, and revolution—life for my father and his family was unimaginably hard, and survival was always in question. Consequently, my father's definition of a relationship was a working partnership in which marriage was a means of survival, similar to the recruitment of mail-order brides by hardscrabble pioneers who homesteaded the Wild West in the 1800s.

My parents' marriage echoed my father's "business first" attitude even though my mother, who was born in America, did not share his philosophy. My mother and father worked together six days a week in a successful family business, but none of their children can recall seeing them share a kiss or a romantic moment. As I entered my early teens, the dissolution of their marriage became apparent when my mother's anger over a loveless relationship exacerbated my father's drinking. My younger brother and sister and I hid in our closets as frequent verbally abusive arguments shattered our formerly peaceful home. When my father and mother finally decided to live in separate bedrooms, an uneasy truce prevailed.

As many conventionally unhappy parents did in the 1950s, my parents stayed together for the sake of the children—they divorced after my youngest brother left home for college. I only wish they had known that modeling their dysfunctional relationship was far more damaging to their children than their separation would have been.

At the time, I blamed my father for our dysfunctional family life. But with maturity I came to realize that both of my parents were equally responsible for the disaster that sabotaged their relationship and our family harmony. More important, I began to see how their behavior, programmed into my subconscious mind, influenced and undermined my efforts to create loving relationships with the women in my life.

In the meantime I experienced years of pain. The dissolution of my own marriage was emotionally devastating, especially because my two wonderful daughters, now loving and accomplished women, were just little girls. It was so devastating that I vowed never to marry again. Convinced that true love was a myth—at least for me—every day for 17 years I repeated this mantra when I shaved: "I won't get married again. I won't get married again."

Needless to say, I wasn't committed-relationship material! But despite my morning ritual, I couldn't ignore what is a biological imperative for all organisms, from

single cells to our 50-trillion-celled bodies—the drive to connect with another organism.

The first Big Love I experienced was a cliché: an older man with a bad case of arrested emotional development falls in love with a younger woman and experiences an intense, hormone-driven, teenage-style affair. For a year I floated happily through life high on "love potions," the neurochemicals and hormones coursing through my blood that you'll read about in Chapter 3. When my teenage-style love affair inevitably crashed and burned (saying she needed "space," she rode her bicycle a very short space away into the arms of a cardiovascular surgeon), I spent a year in my big, empty house wallowing in pain and pining for the woman who had left me. Cold turkey is horrible, not just for heroin addicts but also for those whose biochemistry reverts to everyday hormones and neurochemicals in the wake of a failed love affair.

One cold Wisconsin winter day I was sitting alone (as usual), ruminating again about the woman who had left me. I suddenly thought, *Goddammit, leave me alone!* A wise voice that occasionally appears at pivotal times of my life responded, "Bruce, isn't that exactly what she did?" I burst out laughing and that broke the spell. From then on, any time I started obsessing, I would laugh. Finally, I had gotten past withdrawal through laughter, though I still had a long way to go to get my act together!

How far I was from getting my act together became crystal clear to me when I moved to the Caribbean to teach at an offshore medical school. I was living in the most beautiful place on Earth in a villa by the ocean with gorgeous, sweet-smelling flowers; the villa even came with a gardener and a cook. I wanted to share my new life with someone (though of course not get married—I was still fixated on my morning mantra). I wanted more than a sexual partner. I wanted someone I could share my new life with in the most beautiful place on Earth. But the harder I looked, the less I found, even though I had what I thought was the world's best pickup line: "If you're not doing anything, how about hanging out with me at my Caribbean villa?"

One night I tried what should have been my surefire pickup line on a woman who had just arrived on Grenada, the picture-perfect island I had come to love. We went to the yacht club bar and chatted. I thought she was interesting, so I asked her to stay for a while instead of going back to her job working on a yacht. She looked me in the eye and said, "No, I could never be with you. You're too needy." The bullet hit—I was blown back into my chair in silence. After a long, stunned moment, I recovered my speech and managed to say, "Thank you. I needed to hear that." Not only did I know she was right; I knew that I needed to get my own life together before I could have the truly loving relationship I so desperately wanted.

Then a funny thing happened: as soon as I let go of my desperate quest for a relationship, women who wanted a relationship with me started to appear in my life. Finally, the true inspiration for this book, my beloved Margaret, entered my life and we started living our lives like those portrayed in the romantic comedies I once dismissed as fantasy.

But that's getting ahead of the story. First I had to learn that I was not "fated" to be alone, that I was not "fated" to have to settle for a series of failed relationships.

I had to learn that not only had I *created* every failed relationship in my life, I could *create* the wonderful relationship I wanted!

The first step began in the Caribbean when I experienced the scientific epiphany I described in my first book, *The Biology of Belief.* While mulling over my research on cells, I realized that cells are not controlled by genes and neither are we. That eureka instant was the beginning of my transition, as I chronicled in that book, from an agnostic scientist into a Rumi-quoting scientist who believes that we all have the capacity to create our own Heaven on Earth and that eternal life transcends the body.

That instant was also the beginning of my transition from a marriage-phobic skeptic into an adult who finally took responsibility for every failed relationship in his life and realized he could create the relationship of his dreams. In this book, I'll chronicle that transition using some of the same science outlined in *The Biology of Belief* (and more). I'll explain why it is not your hormones, your neurochemicals, your genes, or your less-than-ideal upbringing that prevents you from creating the relationships you say you want. Your *beliefs* are preventing you from experiencing those elusive, loving relationships. Change your beliefs, change your relationships.

Of course, it's more complicated than that, because in relationships between two people there are actually four minds at work. Unless you understand how those four minds can work against one another, even with the best of intentions, you'll be "looking for love in all the wrong places." That's why self-help books and therapy so often foster insight but not actual change—they only deal with two of the four minds at work in relationships!

Think back to the most spectacular love affair of your life—the Big One that toppled you head over heels. You made love for days on end, didn't need food, barely needed water, and had endless energy: it was the Honeymoon Effect that was to last forever. So often, though, the honeymoon devolves into daily bickering, maybe divorce, or just tolerance. The good news is that it doesn't have to end that way.

You might think that your Big Love was a coincidence at best or a delusion at worst, and that the collapse of your Big Love was bad luck. But in this book, I'll explain how you created the Honeymoon Effect in your life and its demise as well. Once you know how you created it and how you lost it, you can, like me, quit whining about your bad karma in relationships and create a happily-ever-after relationship that even a Hollywood producer would love.

After decades of failure, that's what I finally manifested! Because so many people have asked how we did it, Margaret and I will explain in the Epilogue how we've managed to create our happily-ever-after Honeymoon Effect for 17 years and counting. We want to share our story because love is the most potent growth factor for human beings, and love is contagious! As you'll find when you create the Honeymoon Effect in your own life, you'll attract similarly loving people to you—and the more the merrier. Let's take Rumi's eight-centuries-old advice and revel in our love for one another so this planet can finally evolve into a better place where all organisms can live their own Heaven on Earth. My hope is that this book will launch you on a journey, as that instant in the Caribbean launched me, to create the Honeymoon Effect each and every day of your life.

CHAPTER 1

Our Drive to Bond

It is beyond our imagination to conceive of a single form of life that exists alone and independent, unattached to other forms.

—Lewis Thomas

If you're a survivor of multiple failed relationships, you may wonder why you keep trying. I can assure you that you don't persist just for the (sometimes short-lived) good times. And you don't persist because of TV ads featuring loving couples on tropical islands. You persist, despite your track record and despite dismal divorce statistics, because you are designed to bond. Human beings are not meant to live alone.

There is a fundamental biological imperative that propels you and every organism on this planet to be in a community, to be in relationship with other organisms. Whether you're thinking about it consciously or not, your biology is pushing you to bond. In fact, the coming together of individuals in *community* (starting with two) is a principle force that drives biological evolution, a phenomenon I call *spontaneous evolution,* which I cover in depth in the book of the same name.[1]

There are, of course, additional biological imperatives designed to ensure individual and species survival: the drive for food, for sex, for growth, for protection, and the ferocious, inexplicable drive to fight for life. We don't know where or how the will to live is programmed into cells, but it is a fact that no organism will readily give up its life. Try to kill the most primitive of organisms and that bacterium doesn't say, "Okay, I'll wait until you kill me." Instead, it will make every evasive maneuver in its power to sustain its survival.

When our biological drives are not being fulfilled, when our survival is threatened, we get a feeling in the pit of our stomach that something is wrong even before our conscious minds comprehend the danger. That gut feeling is being felt globally right now—many of us are feeling that pit in our stomach as we ponder the survivability of our environmentally damaged planet and of the human beings who have damaged it. Most of this book focuses on how individuals can create or rekindle wonderful relationships, but in the final chapter I'll explain how the energy created by "Heaven on Earth" relationships can heal the planet *and* save our species.

That's a tall order, I know, but we have at hand an extremely successful model for creating healing relationships that will ultimately lead to the healing of our planet. As the ancient mystics have said, "The answers lie within." The nature and power of harmonious relationships can be seen in the community of the trillions of cells that cooperate to form every human being. This

might at first seem strange to you because when you look in the mirror, you might logically conclude that you are a single entity. But that is a major misperception! A human being is actually a community made up of 50 trillion sentient cells within a skin-covered petri dish, a surprising insight I'll explain further in Chapter 3.

As a cell biologist, I spent many hours happily studying the behavior and fate of stem cells in plastic culture dishes. The trillions of cells within each skin-covered human body live far more harmoniously than feuding couples and strife-ridden human communities. This is one excellent reason why we can learn valuable insights from them: 50 *trillion* sentient cells, 50 *trillion* citizens living together peacefully in a remarkably complex community. All the cells have jobs. All the cells have health care, protection, and a viable economy (based on an exchange of ATP molecules, units of energy biologists often refer to as the "coin of the realm"). In comparison, humanity's job—figuring out the logistics of how a relatively measly seven *billion* humans can work together in harmony—looks easy. And compared to the 50-trillion-celled-cooperative human community, each couple's job—figuring out how *two* human beings can communicate and work together in harmony—seems like a piece of cake (though I know that at times it seems like the hardest challenge we face on Earth).

I grant you that single-celled organisms, which were the first life forms on this planet, spent a lot of time —almost three billion years—figuring out how to bond with one another. Even I didn't take that long! And when they did start coming together to create multicellular life forms, they initially organized as loose communities, or "colonies," of single-celled organisms.

But the evolutionary advantage of living in a community (more awareness of the environment and a shared workload) soon led to highly structured organisms composed of millions, billions, and then trillions of socially interactive single cells.

These multicellular communities range in size from the microscopic to those easily seen by the naked eye: a bacterium, an amoeba, an ant, a dog, a human being, and so on. Yes, even bacteria do not live alone; they form dispersed communities that keep in constant communication via chemical signals and viruses.

Once cells figured out a way to work together to create organisms of all sizes and shapes, the newly evolved multicellular organisms also started to assemble into communities themselves. For example, on the macro level, the aspen tree *(Populus tremuloides)* forms a superorganism made up of large stands of genetically identical trees (technically, stems) connected by a single underground root system. The largest known, fully connected aspen is a 106-acre grove in Utah nicknamed Pando that some experts contend is the largest organism in the world.

The social nature of harmonious multiorganism societies can provide fundamental insights directly applicable to human civilization. One great example is an ant, which, like a human being, is a multicellular social organism; when you take an ant out of its community it will die. In fact, an individual ant is really a suborganism; the true organism is actually represented by the ant *colony.* Lewis Thomas described ants this way: "Ants are so much like human beings as to be an embarrassment. They farm fungi, raise aphids as livestock, launch armies into war, use chemical sprays to alarm and confuse

enemies, capture slaves . . . engage in child labor . . . exchange information ceaselessly. They do everything but watch television."[2]

Nature's drive to form community is also easy to observe in mammalian species, such as horses. Rambunctious colts run around and irritate their parents just as human children can. To get the colts in line, their parents nip their offspring as a form of negative reinforcement. If those little bites don't work, the parents move on to the most effective punishment of all—they force the misbehaving colt out of the group and do not let it return to the community. That turns out to be the ultimate punishment for even the friskiest, least controllable colt, which will do anything in its behavioral capacity to rejoin the community.

As for human communities, we can fend for ourselves as individuals longer than a single ant can, but we're likely to go crazy in the process. I'm reminded of the movie *Cast Away,* in which Tom Hanks plays a man who is marooned on an island in the South Pacific. He uses his own bloody hand to imprint a face on a Wilson Sporting Goods volleyball he calls "Wilson" so he can have someone to talk to. Finally, after four years, he takes the risky step of venturing off the island in a makeshift raft because he'd rather die trying to find someone to communicate with than stay by himself on the island, even though he has figured out how to secure food and drink—that is, how to survive.

Most people think that the drive to propagate is the most fundamental biological imperative for humans, and there's no doubt that reproduction of the individual is fundamental to species survival. That's why for most of us sex is so pleasurable—Nature wanted to ensure that humans have the desire to procreate and sustain the species. But Hanks doesn't venture off the island to propagate; he ventures off the island to communicate with someone other than a volleyball.

For humans, coming together in pairs (biologists call it "pair coupling") is about more than sex for propagation. In a lecture entitled "The Uniqueness of Humans," neurobiologist and primatologist Robert M. Sapolsky explains how unique humans are in this regard:

> Some of the time, though, the challenge is we're dealing with something where we are simply unique—there is no precedent out there in the animal world. Let me give you an example of this. A shocking one. Okay. You have a couple. They come home at the end of the day. They talk. They eat dinner. They talk. They go to bed. They have sex. They talk some more. They go to sleep. The next day they do the same exact thing. They come home from work. They talk. They eat. They talk. They go to bed. They have sex. They talk. They fall asleep. They do this every day for 30 days running. A giraffe would be repulsed by this. Hardly anybody out there has non-reproductive sex day after day and nobody talks about it afterward.[3]

For humans, sex for propagation *is* crucial until a population stabilizes. When human populations reach a state of balance and security, sex for propagation decreases. In the United States, where most parents expect their children to survive and also expect that they themselves won't be out on the streets with a cup when

they're old, the average number of offspring per family is fewer than two. However, any population that is threatened will initiate reproduction earlier and reproduce more—they're unconsciously doing the calculation that some of their children are not going to survive and that they'll need more than two children to share the load of helping to support them when they're old. In India, for example, though the fertility rate dropped 19 percent in a decade to 2.2, in the poorest areas where families face tremendous challenges to survive, the rate can be three times higher.

But even in societies where the drive to reproduce is curtailed, there is still an incentive for coupling because the drive to bond trumps the drive to procreate. Couples who don't have children can create wonderful relationships, and many make a conscious decision not to have children. In *Two Is Enough: A Couple's Guide to Living Childless by Choice,* author Laura S. Scott explores why some forgo the experience. Scott starts off the book with a conversation with a friend's husband, who was at the time a new dad:

> "So why did you get married if you didn't want kids?" Huh? Love . . . companionship, I blurted. His question startled me, rendering me uncharacteristically short of words . . . He cocked his head and waited for more, his curiosity genuine. In that moment, I recognized just how strange I must have seemed to him. Here was a person who could not imagine life without kids trying to understand a person who could not imagine a life *with* kids.[4]

Scott started researching the subject and found that according to a 2000 Current Population Survey, 30 million married couples in the United States do not have children and that the United States Census Bureau predicted that married couples with children would account for only 20 percent of households by 2010.[5] Scott also did her own survey of couples who are childless by choice and found that one important motive for not having children was how much the couples valued their relationships. Said one of the surveyed husbands, "We have a happy, loving, fulfilling relationship as we are now. It's reassuring to think that the dynamic of my relationship with my wife won't change."[6]

Perhaps if more people realized that coupling in higher organisms is fundamentally about bonding, not only about the drive to reproduce, there would be less prejudice against homosexuality. In fact, homosexuality is natural and common in the animal kingdom. In a 2009 review of the scientific literature, University of California at Riverside biologists Nathan W. Bailey and Marlene Zuk, who advocate more study about the evolutionary impetus for homosexual behavior, state, "The variety and ubiquity of same-sex sexual behavior in animals is impressive; many thousands of instances of same-sex courtship, pair bonding and copulation have been observed in a wide range of species, including mammals, birds, reptiles, amphibians, insects, mollusks, and nematodes."[7] One example is silver gulls; 21 percent of female silver gulls pair with another female at least once in their lifetimes and 10 percent are exclusively lesbian.[8]

Since we're driven to form bonds, whether they are homosexual or heterosexual, we need to understand how

Nature intended us to bond, which is the topic of this book. Until we successfully learn how to couple, how can we follow the example of cells to create larger cooperative communities? Until we successfully learn how to couple better, the next stage of our evolution, wherein humans assemble to form the larger superorganism *humanity,* is stalled. If ants can do it, so can we humans!

The good news is that the story of evolution is not only a story of the survival of cooperative communities but also a story of repeating patterns that can be understood through geometry, the mathematics of putting structure into space. Humans didn't create geometry—they derived it from studying the structure of the Universe because it provides a way of understanding the organization of Nature. As Plato wrote, "Geometry existed before creation."

The repeating patterns of the new geometry, *fractal geometry,* reveal a surprising insight into the nature of the Universe's structure. Even though we know in the pit of our stomach that we are at a crisis point, fractal geometry makes it clear, as I'll explain later, that the planet has been in dire straits before. Each time, though there were casualties along the way (most notoriously dinosaurs), something better emerged out of the crisis.

The mathematical computations involved in fractal geometry are actually quite simple; equations use only multiplication, addition, and subtraction. When one of these equations is solved, the answer is reinserted into the original equation and solved again. This "recursive" pattern can be repeated infinitely. When fractal equations are repeatedly solved more than a million times (computations made possible by the advent of powerful computers), visual geometric patterns emerge. It turns out that an inherent characteristic of fractal geometry is the creation of ever-repeating, "self-similar" patterns nested within one another. The traditional Russian matryoshka doll provides a great image for understanding fractal patterns. A symbol of motherhood and fertility, the doll is actually a set of wooden dolls of decreasing size that nest into each other. Each doll is a miniature though not necessarily exact replica of the larger ones.

Just like Russian nesting dolls, the repeating patterns in Nature make its fractal organization clear. For example, the pattern of twigs on a tree branch resembles the pattern of limbs branching off the trunk. The pattern of a major river is similar to the patterns of its smaller tributaries. In the human lung, the pattern of branching along the large bronchus airway is repeated in the smaller bronchioles. No matter how complicated organisms are, they display repetitive patterns.

These iterative patterns help make the natural world more comprehensible. Despite the evolution of increasing complexity in the structure of cooperative multicellular communities, the amazing fact is that in the physiology of humans—the organisms that are presumably at the top of the evolutionary ladder—there are no new functions that aren't already present in simple cells at the bottom of the evolutionary ladder. Digestive, excretory, cardiovascular, nervous, and even immune systems are present in virtually all of the single cells that comprise our bodies. Show me a function in your human body and I'll show you where it originally arose in the single cell. These repeating fractal patterns mean that everything we learn from Nature's simple organisms applies to more complex organisms as well as to us humans. So if you want to understand the nature of the Universe, you don't have to take on the whole thing—you can study its components as I did when I was a cell biologist. Fractal geometry's repeating patterns provide a scientific framework for the principle that mystics call "as above, so below." We are clearly *part of* the Universe, not an add-on afterthought whose job is to "conquer" Nature.

A biosphere built on the repetitive patterns of fractal geometry also offers an opportunity to predict the future of evolution by looking back on its history. In contrast, conventional Darwinian theory holds that evolution is *initiated* by random mutations, genetic "accidents," which implies that we cannot predict the future. But following in the footsteps of cells, our future *should be* one of more and more cooperation and more and more harmony so that humans (starting with pair-bonded twos) can learn to cooperate to form the larger evolved communal organism defined as humanity.

Instead of cursing our bad luck in relationships, we need to recognize that our efforts at bonding are a fundamental drive of Nature and that these bonds can be cooperative and harmonious. We need to heed Rumi's sage advice: "Yesterday I was clever, so I wanted to change the world. Today I am wise, so I am changing myself." When we start living in harmony with Nature (and with ourselves), we can move on to creating the Honeymoon Effect in our lives, where relationships are based on love, cooperation, and communication. In the next chapter, we'll explore the most fundamental form of communication among organisms: energy vibrations.

CHAPTER 2

Good Vibrations

I believe that there is a subtle magnetism in Nature, which, if we unconsciously yield to it, will direct us aright.

—Henry David Thoreau

I was living in paradise, away from the legal and financial battles that had engulfed my life, when I made a mistake no self-respecting nonhuman mammal would ever make. Does a gazelle hesitate when he/she senses the presence of a lioness? Does the gazelle amble over to her and ask, "Are you my friend?" Of course not. As soon as the gazelle senses a lioness's presence, the gazelle makes tracks at a phenomenal speed—up to 50 miles per hour—to avoid becoming dinner.

But when a human predator who made my skin crawl moved in two doors from me, what did I do? Take the olive-greenish tint of his skin as a warning? Take the uh-oh-there's-no-escape-in-this-dark-alley pounding of my heart as a warning? Take the image of a devil that invariably came to me when I saw him as a sign to stay away?

No. Instead, I worked very hard to talk myself out of my visceral abhorrence of him. After all, I was transitioning from agnostic professor to enlightened spiritual scientist. I was focusing on positive thinking, which meant I didn't want to think about or acknowledge the reality of human predators. I was also trying to focus on forgiveness. In addition to looking devilish to me, this man's physical appearance was very similar to that of a man who had dragged me into a court battle, someone I thought at the time might turn around if I focused on forgiving him. (Short story. In this case it hasn't worked yet.) I struggled with my abhorrence by engaging in idle conversation with him—I worked at being verbally civil and succeeded. My mind rationalized the angst I felt every time I saw him, viewing it as some form of New Age penance.

About a year after I met my predator neighbor, the movers arrived to pack up my stuff for my move from Barbados to Grenada. When the medical school where I was teaching had transferred me, I thought my beneficence had been rewarded in two ways. First and foremost, I was thrilled that I would never again have to see the man who still made my skin crawl. Second, I thought that my instincts must have been wrong because he showed up to help load *all* my possessions (minus one suitcase for a quick trip back to the States), including my beloved high-end photography equipment, onto the delivery truck. *He wasn't such a bad guy after all,* my rational mind was telling me. All the while, my still erratically behaving heart wanted to escape!

The truth came crashing down when I flew back to the Caribbean and learned (after badgering the movers for several days) that my stuff was never going to arrive. My predator neighbor had gone to the delivery company's office the day after I left Barbados, canceled the shipment, gotten a refund of *my* money, stolen all my stuff, and then vanished from Barbados. What was supposed to be a lesson in forgiveness and positive thinking ended up being a lesson in how to deal with the loss of everything I owned. Again. That was the fourth and, I hope, final time I lost all my possessions. Yes, I have had an eventful life!

More important for this chapter, the loss of all my possessions was a painful lesson for me about the importance of trusting "bad vibes" and "good vibes." All organisms on this planet use vibration (aka energy) as a primary means of communication. I learned the hard way that ignoring this primary means of communication is a huge mistake, one we humans make all the time. Essentially, we buy the Brooklyn Bridge even though on some level we *know* we're being had. We override our *feelings* when our rational minds focus on *words,* especially when they're spoken by silver-tongued swindlers (or lovers).

The problem with words, as much as I love them, is that they can cover up far more reliable energetic communication. I once heard a line of dialogue in a movie at 3 A.M., just as I was starting to doze off, a line memorable enough to make me happy I had stayed up half the night: "Language was designed to hide feelings." There was nothing my predator neighbor had *said* that would have tipped me off to his chosen career as a scam artist. There was nothing I *said* that would have tipped him off to the fact that I was on to him. Yet as much as I tried to *talk* myself out of it, on some level I *knew* because I could read his energy, his bad vibrations.

To create the Honeymoon Effect in your life, you'll need to take advantage of your wonderful innate gift, the ability to sense good and bad vibrations. And to do so you'll likely have to overcome the programming you received in your youth, although that's not the only programming you'll have to undo, as I will explain in Chapter 4.

So many of us learned from a young age to ignore messages we receive energetically: "Don't listen to your feelings. Listen to the words." So we talk ourselves out of what we know viscerally/energetically. We ignore warnings signs like *He's lying when he says he loves me.* We feel guilty (as I did about my strong dislike for my neighbor) so we rationalize, telling ourselves, *I must be wrong because he's saying all the right things, and, after all, I love him and love conquers all.* Or we ignore good vibrations. *She's really great, but it would never work out because she's not my type.*

If "reading" energetically transmitted messages sounds like woo-woo New Age speak to you, it's not. Actually it's mainstream quantum physics—and yes, we've now come to the real topic of this chapter! At one time reading others' energy would have sounded woo-woo to me. Like most biologists of my generation, I accepted the principles of Newtonian physics that brilliantly measure and describe how the *material* universe works. When Newton showed that he was able to predict the movements of the solar system by using physical data only, leaving God out of the equation, a rift opened up between science and religion. By the time I was studying

science, that rift had become enormous. Until recently, life scientists generally focused on studying the physical realm and left the invisible realm to followers of religion, of which I was not one.

In retrospect, I can see that other scientists and I were incredibly naive to think that the mechanics of the Universe could be explained using only hyperrational, traditional, Newtonian physics. As accurate as Newtonian principles are for the material world, they are just not enough to explain this world that includes good and bad vibes, miraculous remissions of disease, psychic communication, and the Honeymoon Effect.

Like most biologists, I was slow to adapt to the post-Newtonian world. When I finally grappled with quantum physics, I realized that Max Planck, Werner Heisenberg, my childhood hero Albert Einstein, and other pioneering thinkers have given us a new physics that offers us a window on forces that we can't see but that are truly the stuff of life.

What quantum physics teaches us is that everything we thought was physical is *not* physical. Instead, everything in this Universe is made out of immaterial energy, and everything radiates energy. It is a given fact of science that every atom and every molecule both radiates and absorbs light (energy).[1] Because all organisms are made out of atoms and molecules, you and I and every living thing are radiating energy ("vibes"). That includes my predator neighbor who was radiating the kind of energy I should have known to avoid!

But, you protest, doesn't the fact that you regularly stand on a stage and lecture about the Honeymoon Effect without falling *through* the stage demonstrate that you're a physical being and that the stage you don't fall through is a material substance?

No and no! On stage, I'm standing on whirling vortices of energy, which is why I don't fall through (though I have fallen *off,* but that's another story). And when you look at me, the fact that you see a physical being is only an illusion. I don't have any physical structure—what you're seeing are photons of light bouncing off me!

Unless you're already knowledgeable about quantum physics, I'm sure I haven't convinced you to give up your belief that we live in a material world. I grant you that the principles of quantum physics are as strange as they are wondrous. So I'll explain as best I can how it can be that the world we once thought of as material is actually energetic.

Originally, Newtonian physics held that the atom was the smallest particle of the Universe. In fact, the word *atom* comes from the Greek *uncuttable.* However, the year 1895 marked the beginning of a renaissance in physics that would forever change our understanding of the world. It was at this time that physicists began to discover that atoms are made up of even smaller particles. Electrons were discovered first, followed by protons and neutrons. These fundamental subatomic particles were then found to be made up of a gaggle of even smaller and strangely behaving particles that include bosons, fermions, and quarks. The discovery of these even smaller subatomic particles opened up the new quantum realm, whose weird characteristics confounded the traditional principles of Newtonian physics.

The weirdest characteristic of quantum physics is that these smaller subatomic particles are not made of matter—they are not physical at all. I love showing the following image of the Newtonian atom versus the quantum atom.

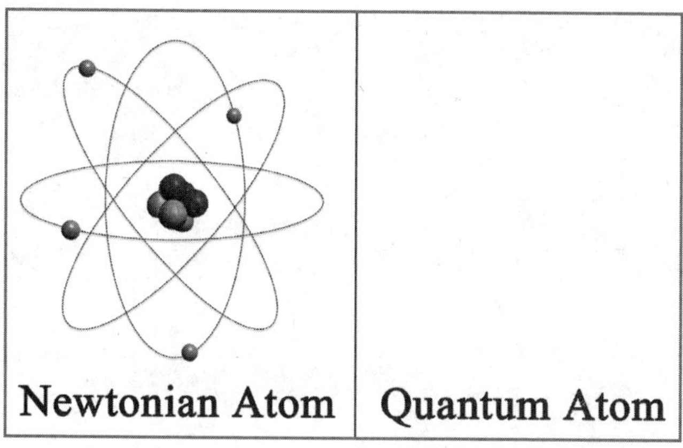

The Newtonian atom on the left can easily be illustrated in a concrete manner using marbles and ball bearings—it's the solar-system-like model on the left that you'll recognize from school textbooks. The illustration of the "quantum atom" on the right looks like a mistake—it's blank. That's because quantum physicists have learned that there is no physical substance inside atoms; the subunits that comprise atoms are made out of extremely powerful invisible energy vortices, the equivalent of nanotornados, not tangible matter. Matter, as it turns out, is a strange form of energy: it is not physical.

For those (including scientists) used to thinking of this world as a material one, it's a hard concept to get your head around. It may help to visualize the energy comprising an atom as a tornado headed toward you as you speed your Porsche down an open highway. The reason you see the tornado as a physical structure in the illustration below is because of the dust and rubble caught up in its whirlwind.

Filter all the dirt and debris out of the tornado, and as is revealed in the image on the right, it would have no physical structure at all; it is "only" an invisible energy force field. But just try to continue your joyride at 100 mph (or less) through the tornado's energy field and you'll experience its force firsthand. Your attempt to drive through the tornado would be as disastrous and fatal as crashing into a stone wall because the tornado's energetic force resists opposing forces (the speeding Porsche), just as physical matter (the wall) does. In fact, the forces generated by atomic "nanotornados" are significantly more powerful than those generated by Hurricane Katrina. These forces are the reason why, when I'm on stage, I don't fall through. I'm standing on whirling vortices of the trillions of atomic nanotornados beneath my feet.

So let's follow this understanding of atoms to its logical conclusion. Atoms are made out of vortices of

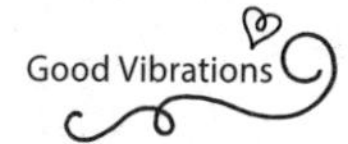

energy. That means molecules, which are made up of atoms, are vortices of energy as well; so cells, which are made up of molecules, are also vortices of energy; and finally, human beings, each of whom is made up of trillions of cells, are . . . *vortices of energy*. It is true that we look as if we are physical, but it is an illusion, a trick of the light—we are all energy!

What does this have to do with our personal lives? Nothing, according to conventional physics courses that suggest that the principles of quantum mechanics apply at only the subatomic level. But some physicists contend as I do that the principles of quantum mechanics have profound implications for our personal lives. Once we accept the fact that we are fundamentally energetic beings inextricably connected to the vast, dynamic energetic field we are part of, we can no longer view ourselves as powerless, isolated individuals who happen to have won the Darwinian evolutionary lottery. Just as mystics throughout history have told us, everything in the Universe is connected: "Enlightenment, for a wave in the ocean, is the moment the wave realizes that it is water," says Vietnamese Buddhist monk Thich Nhat Hanh.

To illustrate the mechanics of the invisible energy field of which we are a part and how those mechanics relate to our lives, I like to use familiar examples from the visible world. When you drop two rocks into a pond, they create ripples, miniature waves. The ripples are not the energy created by the dropped rocks; they are a physical complement of the shape of the invisible energy. The water ripples are created by the force of moving energy (remember the tornado-and-Porsche analogy), which shapes the water as it travels across the surface of the pond.

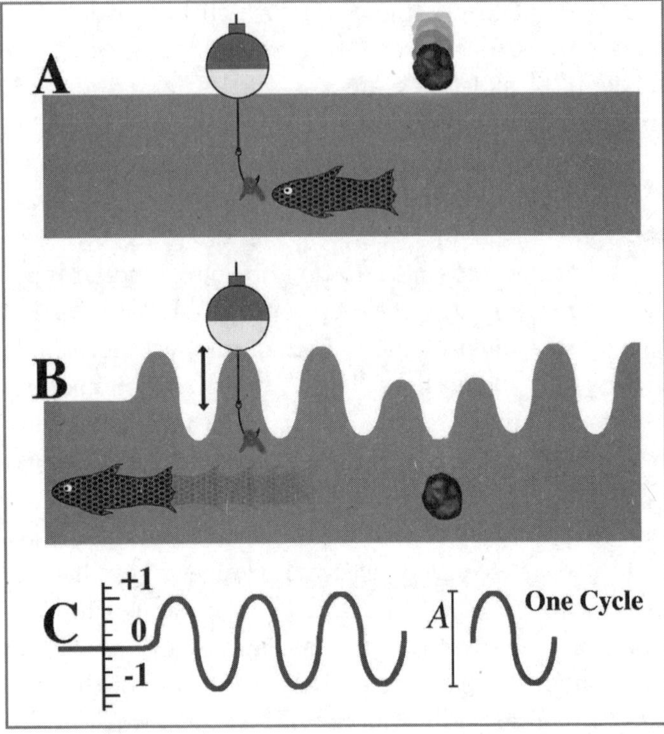

The story of ripples: In Figure A, a fish is contemplating nibbling a worm while a dropped rock is about to hit the surface of the water. After the rock hits the water in Figure B, the rock's kinetic energy is transferred to the water and radiates from the site of impact as a series of concentric ripples. The moving energy shapes the water into miniature waves, but the water itself is not really moving. This is illustrated by the action of the fisherman's bobber, which lifts up vertically and drops down as the waves pass (see arrow). The fact that the bobber does not move horizontally along with the ripples reveals that the water beneath the bobber is not moving. The outline of the ripples reveals the wavelike character of moving energy. Figure C shows the shape of the energy waves. The height and depth of the ripples reflect the power of the energy. The bigger the dropped rock, the more energy it transfers to the water. The power of the energy, measured by the ripple's magnitude, is referred to as the wave's *amplitude* (labeled *A*). The frequency of the energy, measured in hertz, is determined by the number of wave cycles generated per second.

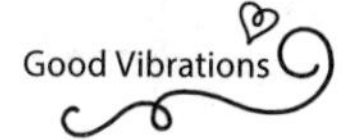

Now let's perform two hypothetical experiments that clearly show how energy interacts. First, drop two rocks of the same size, from the same height, and at exactly the same time into a pond. For this experiment, I'm interested in the point at which the ripples made by each of the two rocks converge. At one point in their convergence, you'll see that the power of the entangled energy waves is amplified because the height of the now combined waves is greater than the heights of the individual ripples that give rise to them. The additive power of the wave produced by two entangled energies, a phenomenon known as *constructive interference* because it amplifies the size of the wave, is illustrated below.

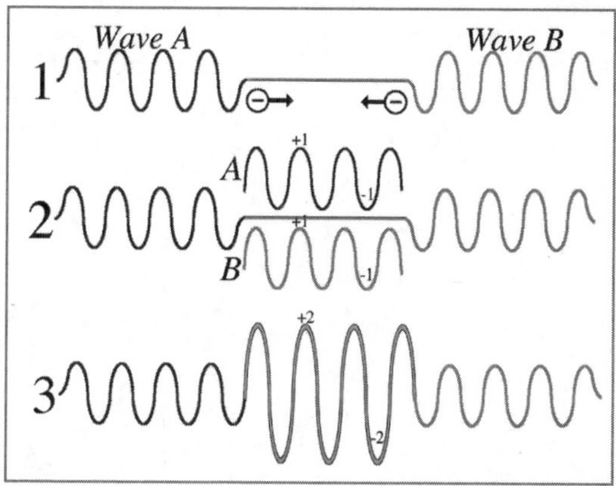

Constructive interference: In Figure 1 above, two sets of ripples are moving across the surface of the water toward each other. As illustrated, both waves A and B are moving toward each other with their ripples *in phase.* In this case, both waves are leading with their negative amplitude. Their cycle patterns are aligned; the waves are *in phase* (harmonic resonance). The waves merge together at the interface where two ripples meet. To illustrate the consequence of this merger, the waves are drawn with one above the other in Figure 2. Where the amplitude of A is +1, the amplitude of B is also +1. Add the two together and the resulting amplitude of the composite wave at that point is +2. Likewise, where A is –1 so is B; together the total amplitude will be –2.

The higher amplitude composite wave illustrated in Figure 3 represents an example of *constructive interference.*

For the second experiment, drop one rock slightly later than its twin. This time you won't see the amplification of energy where you saw it in the first experiment because the energy waves are out of sync—they are not in harmony; when one wave is going up, the other is going down. These out-of-phase energy waves cancel each other out; instead of the energy doubling, it is dissipated and, as you'll see in the following chart, instead of waves rising at the point of convergence, the water is calm there. This phenomenon of canceling energy waves is called *destructive interference* because it diminishes the size of the wave.

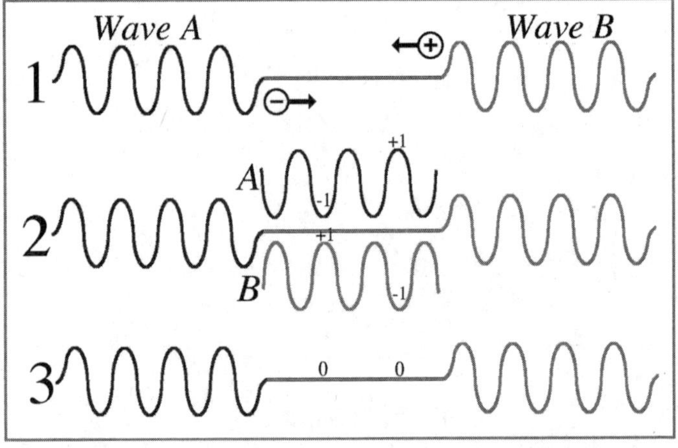

Destructive interference: In Figure 1, the ripples derived from the first rock, labeled as Wave A, are moving from left to right. Wave B, moving right to left, represents the ripples from a second rock dropped shortly after the first. Since the rocks did not hit the water at the same time, the waves will not be aligned when they merge at the interface; they will be *out of phase.* In the illustration, Wave A is leading with a negative amplitude and Wave B is leading with a positive amplitude.

Where they meet in Figure 2, the waves are mirror images of each other; the high amplitude (+1) of one wave is aligned with the low amplitude (-1) of the other, and vice versa. As shown in Figure 3, the amplitude values of each wave cancel each other out, so the composite wave that has 0 amplitude is no wave at all . . . it's flat! The canceled energy waves represent an example of *destructive interference.*

It doesn't take a relationship expert or a quantum physicist to know where I'm going with this. Given the nature of quantum physics, the definition of love—the definition of Happily Ever After—is constructive interference, otherwise known as *good vibes.* Good vibes are nature's way of telling you that you're in the right place or with the right person. Just being in the same room with a partner who is in harmony with you lifts your energy; together you create ripples that produce high-energy waves.

On the other hand, destructive interference, otherwise known as *bad vibes,* is nature's way of alerting you to potential compromising threats. Bad vibes in a relationship may be your nervous system's warning that you're hanging out with the wrong person. An energetically disharmonious relationship likely features shouting matches and recriminations—even being in the same room with your partner depresses you.

So when you "entangle" (quantum physics terminology) with someone else's energy, you want the interference to be constructive (good vibes) not destructive (bad vibes). You want the interaction to *increase* your energy, not *deplete* it. Now that you understand the science behind a phenomenon that you've no doubt already noticed—that some people energize you and some people exhaust you—I hope you'll make it a practice to surround yourself with people who enhance your energy.

Incidentally, as the Chinese figured out long before quantum physicists discovered the influence of the nonmaterial nature of the Universe, you can surround yourself with "physical" objects that enhance your energy as well. Physical objects vibrate just as you do. Feng shui, which originated in Chinese astronomy, balances the physical objects around you in a way that conforms to your energy, thus enhancing qi (energy). To the Western mind, this may seem an odd concept, but you've no doubt already understood its impact without realizing it.

Think about going to a department store for a sale, say a shoe sale at Nordstrom. You find five pairs of shoes you like. They're all the same price and from the same manufacturer, but in different styles. How do you settle on one pair? How do you make your final decision? The answer is that the shoes you actually buy make you *feel* good. They energize you more than the other shoes. You come home with the pair you *love,* not the other shoes you *like.*

Another example is when you visit someone's house and think, *Wow, it's so beautiful—it feels so peaceful. I love this house.* That's a house that resonates well with the energy of its occupants and with your energy as well. Or you visit someone else's house and think, *What's up with that flocked wallpaper? Oh my God, how could they have put that picture on the wall?* That house doesn't match your energy, and its occupants likely don't either.

If I suggest that you go home and read a book, I bet you'll go home and curl up in your *special* chair, the one you feel most comfortable in, even though there may be an identical matching partner parked right next to it. It's not the chair; it's the chair's location in the surrounding energy field that makes you feel good! In the water ripple analogy, the preferred chair is located at the point of the

convergence of the ripples, where they create the most powerful constructive interference.

Or a final example: Have you ever driven your partner crazy by rearranging the furniture or insisting that all the furniture be replaced? The urge to move or replace your furniture is often an indication that you've changed and the furniture's energy field no longer conforms to your new energy field. Or maybe you've *really* changed and you need to move out of the house and away from your partner as well because the house and your spouse are no longer creating constructive interference patterns in your life!

The important point is that you shouldn't let your rational mind discount what your inner voices are telling you . . . whether it's to move your furniture, get rid of a painting that gives you the creeps, bring a new partner into your life, or, in my case, disengage from a neighbor who makes chills run up and down my spine. If you pay attention to good and bad vibes, you'll enhance your energy, and when you enhance your energy you'll enhance your life. If, on the other hand, you discount the importance of reading good and bad vibrations, you may walk into the proverbial lion's den or even wind up staying there, making the rest of your life miserable.

For humans, that's not enough. With our highly evolved big brains, humans can do more than *read* good and bad vibes—we can *create* good and bad vibes when we broadcast thoughts from our brains. For most people, this is a harder concept to accept than spiritual connectedness, feng shui, and destructive/constructive interference. That's because we're used to the notion that our thoughts reside inside our heads—maddeningly so on sleepless nights haunted by obsessive worrying.

But in truth, our brains broadcast signals outside our heads into the environment and respond to signals from the environment as well. Modern medicine exploits this two-way signaling for diagnostic and treatment purposes. You're no doubt familiar with electroencephalography (EEG), in which sensors and wires are placed on the scalp to read the electrical activity of the brain. Magnetoencephalography does the same thing, except that the probe used to read the brain's electromagnetic activity doesn't even touch the head! This amazingly noninvasive technology, which is used for cognitive research as well as for diagnostic purposes such as locating tumors before surgery, works because the brain generates energy fields *outside* the head.

Another noninvasive medical technology, transcranial magnetic stimulation (TMS), generates a magnetic field outside the head to induce electrical activity in a targeted part of the brain.[2] In a 2003 study, Australian researchers found that when they used TMS to boost the neural activity of the area of the brain active in autistic savants, they could improve the drawing skills of some of their research subjects.[3] In 2000, Yale University researchers found that TMS reduced auditory hallucinations in schizophrenics.[4]

The most common usage of TMS is to treat depression that has been resistant to other therapies. More than 30 published studies have found that TMS can help treatment-resistant depression, which laid the foundation for the Food and Drug Administration's decision to approve the first TMS device for treatment of depression in 2008. In 2012 a study published in *Depression and Anxiety* in the Wiley Online Library confirmed the efficacy of TMS for treatment of major depressive disorder

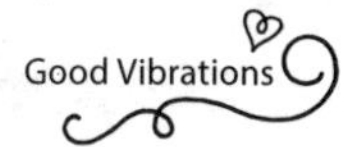

(MDD) in clinical settings. The report, which summarized data collected from 42 clinical TMS practice sites in the United States that treated 307 patients with MDD, found a 58 percent positive response rate among the patients and a 37 percent remission rate.[5]

It is clear from all of these technologies—electroencephalography, magnetoencephalography, and TMS—that the brain generates and responds to energy "fields" that can influence cell behavior and gene expression and alter perception, mood, and behavior. Additionally, the mind's field is responsible for the release and dissemination of neuropeptides and other neurotransmitters that control cell and gene activity. The influence of the mind's field is most evident in the placebo effect, wherein healing is produced by the mind's *belief* that a drug or medical procedure will be effective, even though the drug may only be sugar or chalk or the procedure has no medical value at all.

To truly understand the potential power of our thoughts and beliefs, let's look at another principle of quantum mechanics, "nonlocality," which Einstein memorably called "spooky action at a distance." It turns out that once a quantum particle interacts (or in quantum language, "entangles") with another particle, no matter how many miles apart they are (that is, nonlocal), their mechanical states remain coupled. If, for example, one particle's rotational (tornadolike) spin is clockwise, its entangled twin's rotational spin is the opposite, counterclockwise. Quantum particles also possess a directional polarity, which points either up or down. When one particle's polarity is pointed upward, the polarity of its partner points downward. No matter how much distance separates them, when the polarity or the rotation of one particle's spin changes, the polarity or rotation of its twin changes simultaneously as well, even if one is in Paris and the other is in Beijing.

Physicists have come up with a variety of ingenious stories to help laypeople as well as scientists understand nonlocality, an extremely weird concept for everyone mired in the material world. University of Michigan physicist Luming Duan came up with a quantum casino in which roulette wheels are entangled—if one ball drops down on a black number, the ball at the next table must drop on red.[6]

While physicists established that quantum particles influence each other nonlocally and came up with stories attempting to explain it, parapsychology researchers started looking at whether human minds, like quantum particles, "entangle" nonlocally. Yes, they do! This phenomenon is supported anecdotally by psychics, energy healers, parents, and couples in love who have sensed correctly that something was wrong with an individual, a child, or a partner even though that person was in another city or country.

Theoretical physicist Amit Goswami says that University of Mexico research led him to the "inescapable" conclusion that human minds connect nonlocally: "Quantum nonlocality happens also between brains."[7]

In the University of Mexico experiments, two people meditated next to each other inside an electronically shielded Faraday chamber for 20 minutes with the intention of experiencing a shared meditative state. Then the meditators were placed in two separate chambers, three meters apart in one experiment and 14.5 meters apart in the next experiment, and hooked up to EEG machines. A red light was periodically flashed in the eyes of one

meditator, which induced a unique brain-wave pattern called an "evoked potential." In one out of four cases, the other meditator's brain became "entangled"—it *simultaneously* elicited an evoked-potential brain-wave pattern, even though he/she did not see the light or have any idea the light was being flashed.[8]

Vibrational entanglement is a fundamental component of the "Law of Attraction" and the less talked about, and more personally relevant, "Law of Repulsion," which explain what you bring into your life and what you drive away. I like to illustrate how these laws work with another analogy using familiar objects, in this case a tuning fork and four crystal goblets shown in Figure A on the following page. Each of the four crystal goblets spins at a different frequency, labeled W, X, Y, and Z, because each goblet is made of a different combination of atoms.

Then, in Figure B, I'll strike the tuning fork designed to vibrate at frequency X. Just like the powerful voice of a trained vocalist, the energy vibrations of the tuning fork entangle and constructively interfere with goblet X's atoms, amplifying their energy and causing them to vibrate faster and faster. So much power is created by the energized vibrating atoms that the goblet actually explodes! That's constructive interference of the kind you experienced on your honeymoon when you and your partner's energies were entangling in the best possible way.

By now you're thinking, *If only it were that easy, I'd go out and buy a tuning fork to shape my world!* The good news is that you don't have to buy one; you already have one. The thoughts your brain broadcasts operate as a sophisticated—actually way more sophisticated—tuning fork.

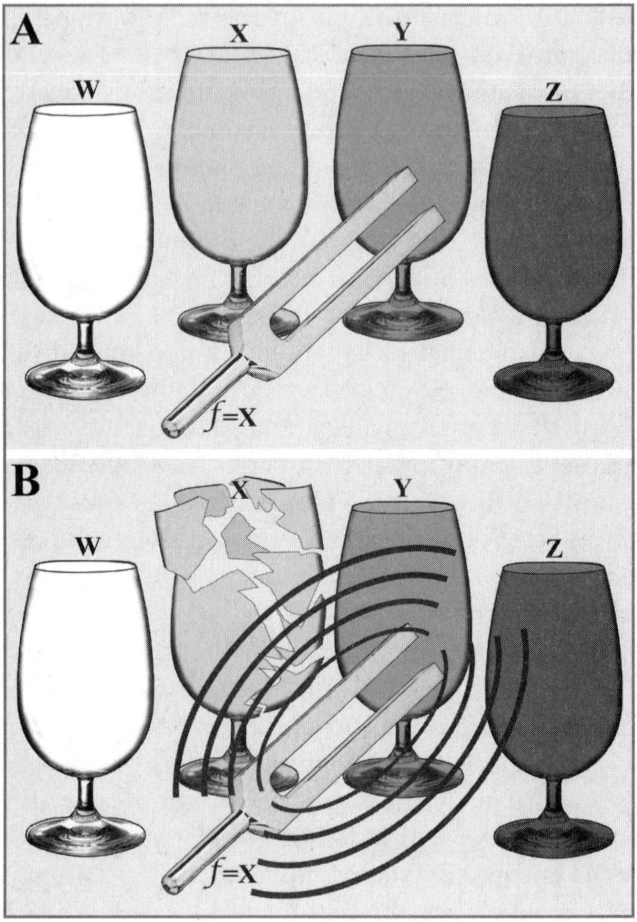

To represent the power of our tuning-fork brain, let's affix images expressing different emotional "energies" to each of the four goblets in the illustration on the next page. Goblet W features a photo of an angry couple, face to face, screaming at each other. Goblet X's photo shows an ecstatic honeymooning couple celebrating a very romantic dinner. Goblet Y illustrates the vexing scenario of *How in the world did I end up with this guy.* Goblet Z's image is of a combative couple blaming each other before a divorce court judge.

Given the choices, it's an easy decision to zero in on goblet X, so let's impact goblet X again, this time using not a visible tuning fork but the thoughts broadcast by your tuning-fork brain. Through constructive interference, your thoughts will energize life experiences that are resonant with the images created by your mind. Focus on goblet X's photo and your emotional exuberance in those days/weeks/months/years when you were in the full throes of Happily Ever After. Forget about the guy who dumped you after you paid his way through law school. Forget about the woman who left you for the dot-com billionaire. Just banish any experiences you've had with the scenes from goblets W, Y, and Z from your thoughts—you don't want to create constructive interference with those images because they'll wind up on your doorstep! While the images represented by goblets W, Y, and Z are not activated by your thoughts, the image in goblet X is. When our thoughts resonate with that image, the harmonious scenario of an ecstatic couple will manifest in our lives.

These goblet analogies illustrate how important it is to shift your passionately negative, fearful, angry thoughts and emotions to passionately positive ones in order to create the Honeymoon Effect in your life. Consider which of the goblet images are most familiar to you and, if the answer is *all but* X, take a look at your thoughts. You can create the life/goblet vision you want by making sure that the thoughts you broadcast reflect exactly what you want to bring into your life. If you're always broadcasting anger about your previous relationships, the same kind of destructive relationship is going to show up at your door again. If you avoid such negative thoughts and images, those scenes will likely not come alive in your life.

Human and animal predators instinctively understand this. Take the example of the lioness I opened this chapter with. Unlike human hunters, the lioness isn't looking for the trophy gazelle with the biggest horns to be mounted on the wall of her den! She is interested in eating. So she does a quick energetic scan of the options and picks the *weakest* gazelle to tangle with, the one she senses will put up the least fight and so provide the fastest, easiest way to get dinner.

When they're not out in the woods hunting for sport, human predators do the same thing. Muggers, for example, look for victims who are broadcasting fearful or distracted energy (sometimes making a mistake and picking the "wrong" victim, who gives them the fight of their lives). It's not the clothes they're wearing—it's the vibrations they're resonating. For all his faults, my predator neighbor was good at one thing: he was a good scam artist because he correctly sensed my weakness; he sensed that I wouldn't definitively turn him away as I should have done. Had I not been broadcasting ambivalent vibrations, he would have moved on to more promising prey.

An interesting series of experiments by parapsychology researcher and anthropologist Marilyn Schlitz, director of the Institute of Noetic Sciences, and British parapsychology skeptic and psychologist Richard Wiseman suggests that the thoughts researchers broadcast play a role even in rigorous scientific experiments. Wiseman and Schlitz collaborated on studies to determine whether a person can detect that someone is staring at them even when they don't see them. These experiments established that when Schlitz was the one doing the staring, there was a statistically significant effect; when Wiseman was the one doing the staring, there was no effect.[9] Those who have read *The Biology of Belief* won't be surprised. The *believer,* Schlitz, started off with the premise that the experiment would work and it did. Wiseman, the *nonbeliever,* started out with the premise that it wouldn't work and of course, as that was *his* belief, it didn't.

Now at this point you might be thinking (negatively), *Well then, no Honeymoon Effect for me because my beliefs are all negative because negative is all I've experienced.* If you're a persistent naysayer, here is some *good* news to stew over. Even if your relationships have been disasters and you're still bitter about them, just fake it for a while. When you shift your thinking to focus on the love, support, and close emotional relationship depicted in goblet X (even if it seems like a scene from a planet unknown to you or from a honeymoon that you experienced once for a week in the distant past), you *can* attract that kind of relationship into your life. You can attract that loving relationship even if you've never experienced one in the past. But if you continue to wallow in the kinds of images and experiences illustrated in the other goblets, they're going to continue to be the only ways you experience relationships.

If this sounds like blaming the victim, it is not. If we have been unaware of how our thoughts and beliefs influence our world, then in truth, how can we be "blamed" or "guilty" for our past actions? There cannot be *blame, guilt,* or *shame* over past events for a fundamental and simple reason: these derogatory words apply *only* when one knows how something works and yet, armed with that knowledge, engages in behavior that is destructive of self or of other "selves."

Clearly, the purpose of presenting the new science is not to give you a reason to wallow in guilt about the past you created. As you now know, wallowing will just attract *more* guilt into your life anyway! The purpose of presenting this information is to help you realize how powerful you really are. Knowledge is power, and with this knowledge you are empowered to create the life and the relationships of your choosing *from now on*. From now on you can embrace and revel in the

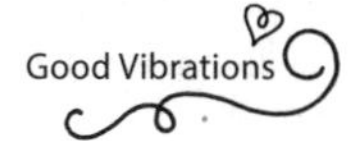

pulsating energetic Universe that Johns Hopkins University physicist Richard Conn Henry posits: "The Universe is immaterial—mental and spiritual. Live, and enjoy."[10]

Live and enjoy the fact that you are a creator, not a victim of your life. You can have the kinds of relationships you want by using your brain as a tuning fork that resonates with what you want to create and avoids thinking about what you don't want to bring into your life. You are manifesting your life. You have the freedom to create what you want to create.

Before I move on to the next chapter, about the biochemistry of love, I'd like to address a good-vibes question that I suspect you may have already thought of. Aren't good vibes about sex, not Happily Ever After love? Though that may be true for organisms lower on the evolutionary ladder, it is not true for humans.

I would be the last person to say sex is bad. Sex is good, even great, and not just for the survival of the species. However, for Happily Ever After the goal is not sex for its own sake. The goal is sex with the person you want to have a real partnership with. As the most evolved animals on the evolutionary ladder, we can do more than just respond to genes and hormones. When you move from bed to bed, from sex to abandonment (I went through that phase), sex becomes like a gymnastic session filled with lots of jumping jacks—and most of us feel there is something missing.

Some argue that because we are closely related to animals lower on the evolutionary ladder, we are not well suited for Happily-Ever-After, monogamous relationships. That's because in the 1990s, when DNA fingerprinting became common, biologists learned that socially monogamous pairs are not necessarily sexually monogamous.

Just like DNA testing that nails absent fathers in child-support cases, research showed that there were lots of missing dads: "The situation has reached the point where *failure* to find extra-pair copulations in ostensibly monogamous species—that is, cases in which monogamous species really turn out to be monogamous—is itself reportable . . ." write David P. Barash and Judith Eve Lipton in *The Myth of Monogamy*.[11]

Consider this Romeo and Juliet–like gazelle story that appeared in an 1847 *Scientific American:*

> A curious instance of affection in the animal, which ended fatally, took place last week at the country residence of Baron Gauci, at Malta. A female gazelle having suddenly died from something it had eaten, the male stood over the dead body of his mate, butting everyone who attempted to touch it, then, suddenly, making a spring, struck his head against a wall, and fell dead at the side of his companion.

In 2011, *Scientific American* reconsidered the 1847 version in a blog item. As lovely as the story is, wrote the second author, it is far more likely that the male gazelle died from the same poison Baron Gauci's female gazelle ingested or from an ill-positioned leap into the wall to avoid what he perceived as a human predator who came too close.[12] The cold, clinical truth is that a male gazelle is not a very likely candidate to sacrifice himself for the love of his life. During mating season, male gazelles mark their territory and mate with *any* mature female who strays into it, though they do draw the line at venturing into a rival gazelle's territory to mate.

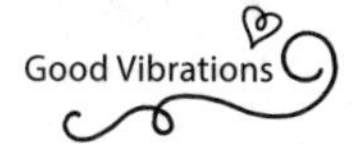

But no matter how many animals bite the monogamy dust (current holdouts include the black vulture, the red-cockaded woodpecker, and the California mouse), I think the big evolutionary leap that our brains enabled sets us apart.

I do grant that at times humans act as if they're nowhere near the top of the evolutionary ladder. I only have to look at incidents in my own life when I acted with less sense than a gazelle. I was in the Caribbean and in my desperately-looking-for-someone phase when I invited a couple, who turned out to be a prototypically dysfunctional pair, to stay at my house on Grenada. Had I taken photos, this couple could have illustrated goblets W, Y, and Z. They were always fighting and screaming, and the yelling alone should have been a tipoff to avoid this particular entanglement. Nevertheless, after their relationship-terminating final and most bitter argument, the woman asked me if I wanted to have sex with her. I ignored all my antennae, rationalized by saying I wasn't breaking up a happy couple, and responded, "Why not?"

I'll tell you why not! I became entangled with this woman's energy in a textbook case of destructive interference. When the woman's former partner left the island, I was the only one left to argue with. I couldn't have been more wrong for her—I'm a nonabusive, nonconfrontational guy. I was driving her mad because she didn't want a better relationship; she wanted a relationship that involved lots of fighting.

As for me, I was drowning in regret. My fear of confrontation limited my options, and I couldn't imagine how to get rid of her. I was living in the middle of the ocean on a little island. Where could she go? The tiny island of Grenada kept getting smaller and smaller, and I became a prisoner in my own house. Maybe Paul Simon wrote "50 Ways to Leave Your Lover" because he lives in metropolitan New York, where it's a lot easier to extricate yourself. In my case, his 50 ways weren't enough. I came up with a 51st way, which was to buy us both tickets to New York—only mine was round trip.

The moral of that story is this: "Be conscious of what you lust for!" I unconsciously *chose* to be driven solely by hormones, and I could have chosen differently. If human beings are just biological machines, lust is going to pull you around (as it did me for a while). When you add consciousness, *you* become the driver of the machine. You are no longer predictable. Even astrologers recognize that when individuals become conscious, astrology isn't as accurate because people become far less predictable. Instead of automatically reacting to the energetic field around us that includes the tides and the pull of planets, we can modify our own vibrations and our responses to the vibrations of others.

So it's time to stop saying I "always" find a guy who's afraid of a commitment or I "always" find a woman who dumps me. We create our lives with our beliefs, and we broadcast those beliefs into the energetic environment around us. We are creating our relationships, and with that knowledge, we have the freedom to create whatever kinds of relationships we want!

If that's so, you might be wondering why my positive thinking about my predator neighbor didn't work. At the time, I was making my first forays into using my brain as a tuning fork, but I still had a lot to learn. Creating the relationship you want is complicated. I didn't

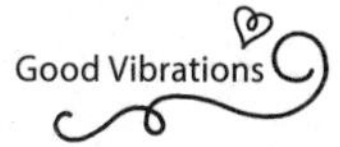

yet fully understand the power of the subconscious to subvert even the best of intentions.

I now know a lot more about how to attract what I want into my life than I did then. I know a lot more about not discounting bad vibes, and I have at long last created a Happily-Ever-After relationship in my life. So despite headlines about spectacularly dysfunctional celebrity marriages, despite plenty of examples of humans allowing their hormones and genes to drive their behavior, it is possible to create a higher level of love. When you acknowledge the power of good vibes and switch your thoughts to goblet X–like images, you will be well on your way to creating Happily Ever After in your life.

CHAPTER 3

Love Potions

Take then this pitcher and remember well my words. Hide it so that no eye shall see nor no lip go near it: but when the wedding night has come and that moment in which the wedded are left alone, pour this essenced wine into a cup and offer it to King Mark and to Iseult his queen. Oh! Take all care, my child, that they alone shall taste this brew. For this is its power: they who drink of it together love each other with their every single sense and with their every thought, forever, in life and in death.

— *The Romance of Tristan and Iseult*
by M. Joseph Bédier

The "essenced wine" spiked with flowers and herbs did its job all too well, as everyone familiar with the tragic, adulterous love story of Irish princess Iseult (also known as Isolde) and Tristan, the Cornish knight who unwittingly drank the brew intended for his uncle King Mark, knows.

Popularized by French medieval poetry, the story of Tristan and Iseult's ill-fated love sparked by an aphrodisiacal brew is just one example of the reputed power of love potions throughout history. Medieval theologian and occultist Albertus Magnus wrote about a concotion of the brains of a partridge calcined into a powder and swallowed in red wine; Galen, the second-century court physician to the Emperor Marcus Aurelius, recommended a glass of thick honey, taken before bedtime, with almonds and one hundred grains of the pine tree; Henry VI favored Amagnac brandy from southwest France; Cleopatra swore by a drink of dissolved pearls in vinegar; and *The Perfumed Garden,* a manual of Arabian erotic technique written in the 16th century by Sheik al-Nefwazi touted a recipe for green peas boiled with onions and powered with cinnamon, ginger, and cardamom seeds, well pounded. Another Arab recipe features the Indian root galanga mixed with cubebs (berries similar to grains of pepper that are indigenous to Java), sparrow wort, cardamoms, nutmeg, gillyflowers, Indian thistle, laurel seeds, cloves, and Persian pepper taken twice daily morning and night in pigeon or fowl broth preceded and followed by water. Least appetizing of all is a recipe cited by the Roman poet Propertius that includes snake bones, a toad, and the feathers of a screech owl.

From the point of view of biochemistry, love is also about potions, but with all due respect to the legend of Tristan and Iseult and the elaborate love potions created throughout human history, the potions I'm talking about are infinitely more sophisticated, finely calibrated neurochemical and hormone cocktails that course through your body when you fall in and out of love.

Yes, what I'm saying is that on one level the Honeymoon Effect is a chemical addiction, which is why things can turn so miserable so quickly when it ends. Watch out if the object of your desire calls it off while you're still basking in your biochemically induced love "high." You might wind up like me, as I described in the introduction, in withdrawal, sitting in a chair in an empty house mooning over your lost love.

In this chapter, I'll talk about the chemicals and hormones that help explain the anxiety, loss of appetite, and euphoria that characterize human love. These chemical love potions spur us on to seek out sexual partners, fixate on a special partner, and bond with that partner long enough to raise the most helpless newborns in the animal kingdom, at least past infancy. Of course it doesn't always work out that way, because this is about humans in love, not about scientific equations—as Shakespeare's fairy Puck famously exclaimed about humans in love: "Lord, what fools these mortals be!"

Before I get into the biochemistry of love, I want to stress that despite Puck's low opinion of foolish mortals in love, we do not have to be slaves to our neurochemicals and hormones! We are "self-biologists" who *create* with the thoughts in our minds the love potions that control the cells and tissues in our bodies. Yes, this is the work of the infamous mind-body connection that until recently has been denied, ignored, or downplayed by conventional science.

Simplifying the Mind-Body Connection

In 1967, I began my first experiments with cloning stem cells. Using a microscope, I scanned cells in a culture dish of mixed cell types, seeking stem cells distinguished by their unique spindle shape. Then I placed a small glass ring around the selected cell, which allowed me to separate it from all the other cells in the dish. Finally, I used enzymes to release the cell from the dish so I could transfer a single stem cell into its own culture dish.

Cells resemble fish in that they live in a water environment; consequently, a tissue culture dish is like a miniature aquarium. Tissue culture medium, a chemically balanced solution that supports growth and viability, provides the cell's environment. Our stem cell culture medium contained a very potent cocktail of salts and nutrients that allowed stem cells to grow and replicate. The single stem cell I added to the culture dish divided about every ten hours in this medium. First there was one cell, then two, then four cells; after a week there were more than 50,000 cells in the dish. Since all of the cells were derived from the same parent cell, all of the cells were genetically identical.

Now here is where the experiment becomes mind-blowing. I split the cell population and placed them into three different culture dishes as illustrated on the next page. Each of the three dishes had a distinct "environment," a culture medium consisting of different biochemicals. In one dish the cells formed muscle, in the second dish the cells formed bone, and in the third dish the cells formed fat.[1a,b]

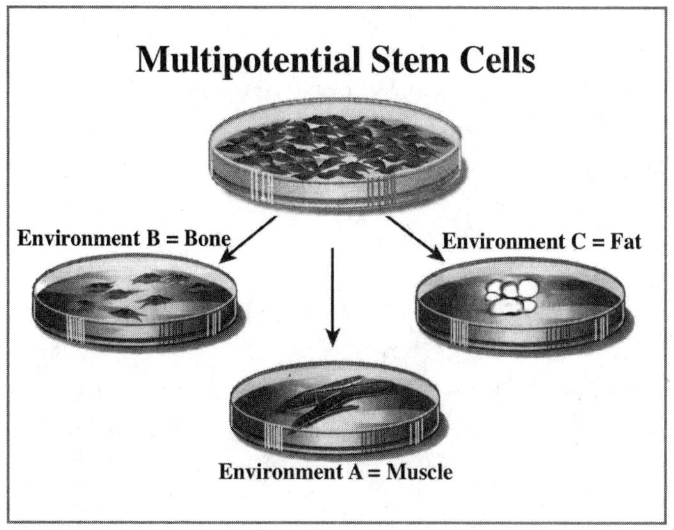

The profound question this experiment answered was this: "What controls the fate of the cells?" Remember, all cells were genetically identical at the start so genes did not control the cells' varying fates! Yes, it was the environment, the culture medium that controlled the expression of the cells. The fate and health of cells are a complement to their environment, a principle I described in *The Biology of Belief* (with a nod to James Carville's advice in Bill Clinton's presidential campaign) as "It's the environment, stupid."

My mentor Irv Konigsberg, one of the first cell biologists to master the art of cloning stem cells, had pointed me in this direction right at the beginning of my career. When I first started cloning cells, he told me that when the cultured cells you're studying are ailing, you look first to the cell's environment, not the cell itself, for the cause: a healthy environment leads to healthy cells; a sick environment leads to sick cells. All of my experiments confirming that "It's the environment, stupid" presaged the now booming field of epigenetics ("above"-genetics), which in study after study is documenting how the environment controls the activity of genes. Finally mainstream science has recognized that genes do *not* determine the fate of cells.

How do these studies relate to you? When you see yourself in the mirror, you see a single human organism—you—looking back. However, as I mentioned in Chapter 1, this is a misperception. We are not single organisms; we are made up of about 50 trillion cells! By strict definition, a human being is a community of living organisms, our cells. More specifically, a human is a "skin-covered" culture dish containing 50 trillion cells. Our blood is the growth medium, the cell-controlling environment within our skin-covered culture dish.

In fact, it makes no difference to the fate of a cell if it is in a *plastic-* or a *skin-covered* culture dish. Wherever it lives, its life is controlled by the culture medium. As a cell biologist, I was responsible for controlling the chemistry of my cells in plastic culture dishes. As a "self-biologist" illustrated in the cartoon on the next page, you control the chemistry of your own culture medium, the blood, through your nutrition and the operation of your brain. When your mind perceives the experience of love, it causes the brain to secrete neurochemicals such as dopamine, oxytocin, and growth hormone into the blood (more on this later). When these chemicals are added to the culture medium of cells grown in a *plastic* dish, the cells react by exhibiting robust, healthy growth. The same occurs for cells in the body's *skin-covered* dish—yes, you are generally healthier and more alive when you're in love.

"Self-Biologist": While the world's population boasts a few cell biologists, the fact is we are all "self-biologists." This cartoon emphasizes that the brain controls the chemistry of the body's culture medium, the blood, which in turn nourishes and regulates the genetics and behaviors of the body's cells. The chemistry released by the brain into the blood complements the perceptions and beliefs we hold in our minds. When we change the way we respond to the world, we change the chemical composition of our blood, which in turn regulates our genetics and behavior. This is the foundation of the placebo effect. (Illustration by Bob Mueller)

However, if the same brain in the same body perceives a threatening world, it does not prompt the brain to release the biochemicals of love. Instead, fear provokes the release of stress hormones and inflammatory agents such as cytokines into the blood. If these chemicals are added to cell cultures in a plastic dish, they cause the cells to stop growing and may cause them to die. The chemistry of stress stunts the growth and maintenance of cells because it diverts the body's energy to support protection mechanisms. This is why stress is the primary cause of illness and is responsible for up to 90 percent of all doctor visits.[2]

It is important to note that stress hormones have multiple roles and their actions are predicated on the type of "stress" an individual is experiencing. There are two types of stress, each with different biochemical consequences: distress and eustress. Distress occurs when we perceive that our survival is threatened. That's when stress hormones like cortisol and adrenaline cause us to shift from growth to protection, saving our lives if there is an acute threat (like a mountain lion) or becoming corrosive if the threat is chronic (like everyday traffic and a job you hate).

Eustress, on the other hand, which literally means "good stress," results when we "stress" the system with nonthreatening behaviors such as engaging in physical activities like sports and mental activities like writing this book, and falling passionately in love! Researchers have found that the stress hormone cortisol is released not just when we're fleeing an avalanche but also when we're blissfully in love. In 2004, University of Pisa researchers found that the levels of cortisol were "significantly higher" among their research subjects who had recently fallen in love than those who were not in love.[3] In 2009, University of Texas researchers found that cortisol levels increased when women in their study were asked to reflect on their romantic partners. The increase was "particularly pronounced and relatively long-lasting" in subjects who spent the most time thinking about their relationships.[4]

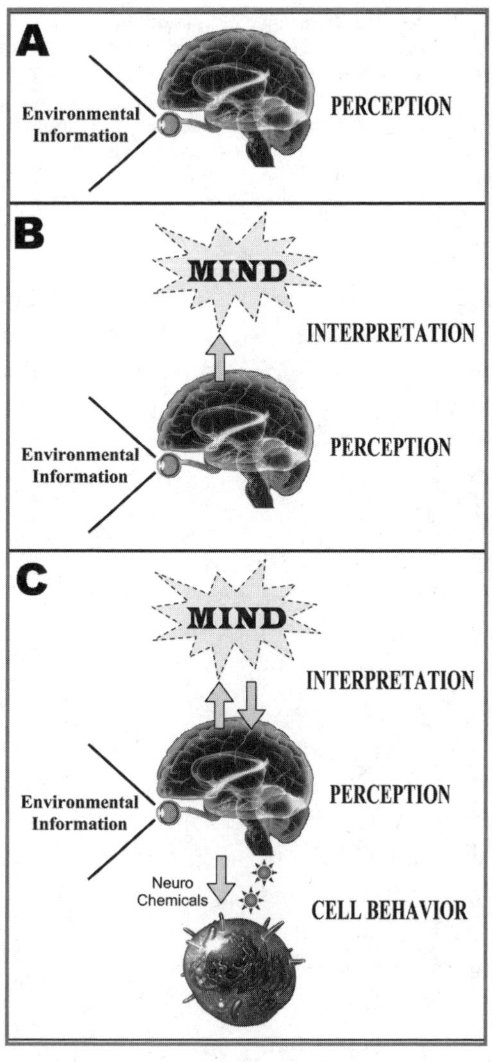

The ABCs of mind-body biology: All living organisms read and respond to environmental information. A: In the process of *perception,* our brains read environmental signals (sights, sounds, smells, temperature, pain, etc.) that are registered by the nervous system's receptors. B: Based upon our instincts and life experiences, the mind assesses the incoming signals and makes an *interpretation,* a value judgment of their meanings as they relate to our survival. C: The mind's interpretation of the incoming signals induces the brain to release neurochemicals that provoke the body to engage in a positive growth response or a life-sustaining protection behavior, or to ignore the signals because they are not relevant to our survival. The neurochemicals released into the blood regulate cell behavior and, via epigenetics, control gene activity.

Whether you're in love or running from danger, your *mind* calibrates your blood's biochemistry, which in turn controls your biology and genetics. The mind interprets your perceptions of the world, and your brain goes to work to produce the biochemistry that complements your perceptions. Here's an example. I love jalapeño peppers; hot, spicy food activates my taste buds in a pleasurable way. But other people see me downing intensely hot food and their reaction is "How can you eat *that?"* Both of us have the same perception—that the food is spicy—but our minds *interpret* those same perceptions differently. My biochemistry revels in jalapeño peppers; yours may reject them.

To better understand the biochemistry of love, think of your brain not as a tuning fork resonating in the Universe's vast energy field, as we did in the chapter on quantum physics. In this context, think of the brain more prosaically as a good old Newtonian machine, actually a paint machine (brains are amazingly versatile—one image isn't enough).

When I say a paint machine, I'm not talking about a robot that flawlessly paints an entire room, including the trim. Would that I had one of those mythical machines! I'm talking about a paint *color mixer* machine that ensures you get *exactly* the hue you want. In these machines, an array of tints is stored in cylinders. The

tints are squirted in precise ratios into a can of white paint to produce the exact shade requested. There is no single red, green, or blue paint. Instead, there are hundreds of variations of each color just as there are in the rainbow spectrum of paint chips that customers use to select their desired wall color.

In our analogy, the brain resembles the paint mixing machine. Rather than blending different color tints, the brain is a *love potion mixing machine* stocked with an array of neurochemicals and hormones that researchers have linked to the biochemistry of love. In the throes of first passion, your brain can order up "passion red" by squirting lots of drops of testosterone into the mix. That went well, so your brain orders up "lovesick pink" with lots of dopamine that motivates the pursuit of more pleasure with the object of your desire. When you're convinced you've found the One your brain orders up love-of-my-life lavender, a mix heavy on the bonding boosters vasopressin, oxytocin, and serotonin, which means you're getting more and more fixated on and obsessed with your True Love. When you defy the divorce/miserable relationship odds and shift into Happily Ever After, the brain mixes up still-crazy-in-love blue with a huge squirt of the cuddle chemical oxytocin.

You get the picture. Our brains have at their disposal a number of ingredients, neurochemical "tints," that can be mixed in varying ratios to produce specific "potions" that compel us first to mate and then to partner with our mates, thereby giving helpless human babies a better chance for survival. Scientists still have a lot to learn about the makeup of these powerful love potions, but here are a few ingredients that have been studied.

Estrogen and Testosterone: Mating

When birds and bees "do it," it is not about falling in love. It is about mating. Take starfish. Female starfish squirt their eggs into the water; males squirt their sperm into the same water. Eventually the twain meet to create another generation of starfish. Not much entanglement there!

Lust-driven human mating requires more entanglement, though long-term partnership doesn't. When it's about lust only, the sex hormones testosterone, notorious for fueling alpha males more interested in sex than bonding, and estrogen, best known for fueling female fertility, play big roles.[5]

Though testosterone is mostly associated with men and estrogen is mostly associated with women, these hormones play reproductive roles in both sexes. Human males produce on average ten times as much testosterone as females and indeed, men with very high levels of testosterone are not ideal partnership material; they tend to divorce more often, abuse their spouses more frequently, and have more affairs than men with less stratospheric levels.[6] But testosterone fuels sexual desire in *both* sexes.[7]

Estrogen soars when females are fertile, and males produce on average only a fraction of the estrogen females produce. But researchers have learned that estrogen plays a role in male sexuality, as well by enabling the maturation of sperm.[8]

My favorite example of the complicated roles estrogen and testosterone play in males and females comes from the bird kingdom: the zebra finch. At one point in its embryonic development, the male zebra finch produces estrogen, which is transformed into a testosteronelike

hormone in the brain, which in turn enables male birds to sing. Male zebra finches begin to sing at puberty, and researchers suspect that just like human females who swoon when their old-fashioned suitors sing outside their balconies, female zebra finches gravitate to their suitors' singing.[9]

The roles estrogen and testosterone play in the male and female reproductive systems are undoubtedly more complex than once thought, but there is no doubt that both help propel us to take the first steps to ensure the survival of our species.

Dopamine: Pleasure and Craving

Testosterone and estrogen may get us to the sex scene, but there's no way we humans would engage in sex with enough frequency and gusto to propagate our species if it weren't pleasurable. Enter the neurotransmitter dopamine, the crucial chemical that fuels the drive to repeat pleasurable experiences. When your dopamine levels are up, you are jazzed: you're not hiding under your blankets alone at home; you're motivated to get out and experience pleasure.[10]

Unsurprisingly, because of its role in driving reproduction, dopamine is an ancient evolutionary molecule. In fact, the role of dopamine in evolutionarily simple organisms, such as microscopic roundworms, is almost identical to its role in humans. That's why University of Texas researchers are able to use genetically modified, dopamine-deficient worms to identify drugs that may help treat Parkinson's disease, which is characterized by a loss of dopamine-producing cells in the brain.[11]

Dopamine is synthesized deep in the brain's ventral tegmental area and released in the nucleus accumbens in the forebrain. These are key areas in the pleasure/reward circuit of our brains, and, as anyone who has struggled with addiction can tell you, this circuit has a dark side. Activated by every variety of pleasurable, potentially addictive substance or activity known to humans—including cocaine, heroin, sex, gambling, shopping, and high-calorie food—too much stimulation can lead to desperate cravings and the risky, compulsive behavior of an addict.[12]

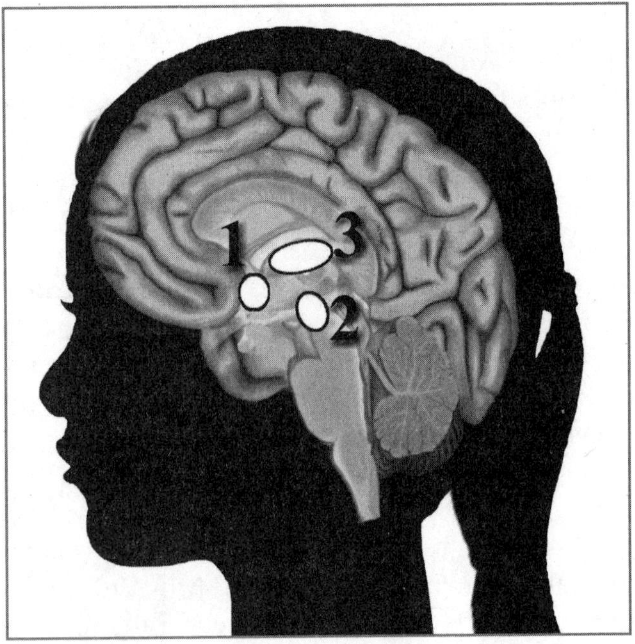

Deep within the center of our brain, specific control centers engage growth and protection behaviors in response to pleasure and pain stimuli. The primary centers include 1: the nucleus accumbens; 2: the ventral tegmentum; and 3: the ventral pallidum.

The sirenlike draw of dopamine has been demonstrated again and again in animals, starting in the 1950s. Rats with electrodes implanted in the part of the brain where dopamine is synthesized press a lever that stimulates their pleasure/reward circuit incessantly—up to seven thousand times per hour. Rats choose stimulation of the pleasure/reward circuit over food and water. Female rats abandon their newborn pups in favor of pressing the lever, mirroring crack addict moms who neglect their children in favor of the drug. The few studies done on humans found the same phenomenon—when given the chance, humans slavishly choose to stimulate the dopamine-producing areas of the brain repeatedly, neglecting relationships and personal hygiene in favor of hits of dopamine.[13]

What does this have to do with the Honeymoon Effect? A number of recent studies have found that it is the reward circuit of the brain that is activated when you're madly in love. These are the very same areas that proved so addictive to rats and a few humans in the laboratory that they ignored everything in favor of jolts of pleasure provided by dopamine-producing areas of the brain.

In 2000, Andreas Bartels and Semir Zeki of University College London recruited 17 madly-in-love students and scanned their brains when they looked at a photo of their beloved and when they looked at a photo of a friend. The pleasure/reward, dopamine-rich circuit of their brains lit up when the students viewed a photo of their beloved and stayed dark when looking at a photo of a friend. Bartels and Zeki concluded, "It is perhaps surprising that so complex and overwhelming a sentiment [love] should correlate differentially with activity in such restricted regions of the brain, and fascinating to reflect that the face that launched a thousand ships should have done so through such a limited expanse of cortex."[14]

Scientists may have been surprised to learn that falling madly in love taps the same brain circuitry as snorting cocaine. However, anyone who's ever sat by the phone waiting for the call, quit a job to follow a lover, or slumped desolate and defeated in a chair with no motivation to leave it after being dumped would not be surprised at all. For lovers who fall head over heels, love can feel like a roller coaster—there can be a fine line between love as "the best thing that's ever happened to me" and, while waiting impatiently and obsessively for the next fix, "the worst thing that's ever happened to me."

Unsurprisingly, given how common divorce and breakups are, researchers say that for most couples the intense roller coaster lasts only a year or two. But that doesn't mean the Honeymoon Effect can't last. When researchers scanned the brains of 17 women and men who reported they were still intensely in love with their spouses after an average of 21 years of marriage, the dopamine-rich areas of their brains associated with reward and motivation lit up just as they do in women and men in the throes of new passion. The researchers wrote, "These data suggest that the reward-value associated with a long-term partner may be sustained, similar to new love."

But the study also found "many more brain regions" involved in long-term intense romantic relationships than in newly-in-love relationships, including areas that are linked to attachment and those that can modulate anxiety and pain. That suggests that long-time romantic

love offers a bonus: "Thus present findings are in line with behavioral observations suggesting that one key distinction between romantic love in its early and later stages is greater calm associated with the latter," concluded the researchers.[15] The pleasure of dopamine combines with the calm that comes with long-term, solid attachment. Sounds like Happily Ever After to me!

Vasopressin: Bonding and Aggression

In most species, females and males do not form what biologists call "pair couples," let alone relationships powerful enough to launch the thousand ships of the Trojan War. In 97 percent of mammals, for example, a male has sex with a female in heat and then goes off to find another female to produce more offspring; the females raise their offspring on their own.

To figure out what makes the 3 percent tick, researchers have extensively studied the prairie vole, a hamster-size rodent from the Midwest. Unlike their promiscuous, relatively asocial cousins, meadow voles, prairie voles form lifelong attachments with their mates, cooperate to rear their offspring, and aggressively protect their nests. When the opportunity presents itself, both male and female prairie voles may stray sexually, but most come back to the partner they've bonded with for life. In fact, field research has found that prairie vole couples beat humans when it comes to long-term pair bonding. Three-quarters of prairie vole couples endure until one dies and even then most do not take on a new mate.[16]

Scientists have zeroed in on two closely related neuropeptides—vasopressin and oxytocin—that are synthesized in the hypothalamus and released in the pituitary to help explain how prairie voles bond so closely. Researchers have found receptors for both molecules in the pleasure/reward regions of the male and female prairie vole, the same regions that light up in brain scans of humans in love. Though vasopressin and oxytocin may play a role in cementing relationships in both males and females, the studies have focused on vasopressin in male prairie voles and oxytocin (more later) in female prairie voles.[17]

Males produce a lot more vasopressin than females, which is why researchers have focused their vasopressin studies on male prairie voles. In animals, vasopressin induces characteristic male behavior like scent-marking of territory and aggression. Hamsters, for example, start scent-marking their territory within a minute of being injected with vasopressin. When the prairie vole ejaculates, his vasopressin levels soar, and he also turns into an attentive partner and parent. Further corroborating the link between bonding and vasopressin, when virgin male prairie voles are injected with vasopressin, they start defending their territory and become instantly possessive of their mates. These studies reveal that vasopressin is linked not just to bonding but also to aggression.[18]

You might expect that the behavioral differences between faithful male prairie voles and philandering male meadow voles could be explained by their differing *levels* of vasopressin (and the more the better), but that is not the case. The key difference between the two voles is the *location* of their vasopressin receptors. Unlike the meadow vole, the monogamous prairie vole's vasopressin receptors are centered in one of the brain's principal pleasure/reward regions, the ventral pallidum, next to the dopamine-rich nucleus accumbens. These regions

are linked to addiction.[19] Researchers have also found the same phenomenon in primates; monogamous marmosets have higher levels of vasopressin bound in the reward centers of their brains than do nonmonogamous rhesus macaques.[20]

Capitalizing on this discovery, researchers at Emory University have turned promiscuous meadow voles into mate- and offspring-loving dads by creating mutant meadow voles with vasopressin receptors in their reward center.[21] And researchers have turned laboratory prairie voles into nonbonding cads by blocking their vasopressin receptors in the lateral septum area of the brain.[22]

Perhaps to the dismay of women with philandering partners, human behavior is too complicated to similarly engineer. Because it's so much harder to study humans, it's too soon to say that human males mimic prairie vole males. But vasopressin is released when humans as well as prairie voles have sex, which provides more evidence that the reward centers of the brain are involved with bonding and love in humans as they are in prairie voles. Scientists are becoming more and more convinced that we can learn a lot from monogamous prairie voles and that at least in males, vasopressin is a key ingredient in the love potions that foster human bonding.

Oxytocin: The Bonds of Love

If biochemistry were simple, which it's not, all you'd need is oxytocin, whose reputation for bonding is clear from some of its nicknames: love drug, cuddle chemical, and trust hormone.

Oxytocin was once known only as the molecule that stimulates uterine contractions during labor, milk production in breast-feeding, and the intense mother-offspring bond in mammals. When oxytocin is injected into the brains of virgin rats, it quickly induces maternal behavior—rat mothers will cross an electrified grid to nurture pups. When oxytocin is blocked, mother rats reject their pups.

But researchers studying female prairie voles discovered that oxytocin promotes bonding with a male partner just as vasopressin promotes male bonding with a female partner. Because their brains are packed with oxytocin receptors in the reward centers and oxytocin levels increase during mating, monogamous female prairie voles learn to associate the feeling of pleasure with their mate (just as humans do). When oxytocin is blocked, famously monogamous female prairie voles do not bond with their mates.[23]

While animal studies laid the groundwork for understanding the importance of oxytocin in couple bonding, it was studies of human couples that turned the molecule into a superstar outside scientific circles.

In one study, Swiss researchers gave 47 couples a nasal spray containing either oxytocin or a placebo. The couples then participated in a videotaped "conflict" discussion. Those who received oxytocin exhibited more positive and less negative behavior and lower levels of the stress hormone cortisol.[24] Other studies suggest that oxytocin promotes trust. In one experiment, research subjects were given a sum of money to invest with a trustee. Half the participants used an oxytocin nose spray before the experiment and the other half a placebo spray. Subjects who received oxytocin were nearly twice as likely to turn all their money over to a trustee.[25] And a National Institute of Mental Health study found

that subjects who inhaled oxytocin before looking at pictures of threatening faces had markedly lower activity in their brains' fear centers.[26]

Unsurprisingly, given its reputation, vendors selling oxytocin nasal spray and sublingual drops have proliferated on the Internet (one product is called "Liquid Trust"). These oxytocin products are marketed to a wide-ranging group of potential consumers, including singles looking for relationships, feuding couples hoping to save their relationships, and salespeople who want people to instantly trust them. But savvy couples cultivating relationships with high levels of trust and comfortable bonding know that, like prairie voles, they can boost oxytocin more pleasurably on their own and without spending a dime through kissing, touching, cuddling, and sex.

Serotonin: Obsession

In 1999, University of Pisa psychiatrist Donatella Marazziti and her colleagues (the same group of researchers that found elevated cortisol levels in subjects madly in love) decided to test the idea that the early stages of romantic love are akin to obsessive-compulsive disorder (OCD). This was an educated guess, given the number of hours people in love report thinking about their partners ("all the time" is not an uncommon estimate) and the number of plaintive love songs with a can't-get-her/him-out-of-my-mind theme.

Marazziti and her colleagues recruited 20 subjects who had fallen in love in the previous six months and spent at least four hours a day thinking about their beloved. They also recruited 20 unmedicated OCD patients and 20 control subjects neither in love nor suffering from OCD. When the researchers tested their subjects' blood, they found that the group suffering from OCD and those in love had similarly low levels of 5-HT, a protein that removes serotonin from between brain cells.

But the researchers also found that the similarities between those in love and those who suffer from pathological OCD were short lived. When the researchers tested the blood of a few of their in-love subjects 12 to 18 months after they first started their relationships, their 5-HT levels had returned to the normal levels of the control group. The results of the experiment, concluded the Pisa researchers, "suggest that being in love literally induces a state which is not normal as indeed suggested by a variety of colloquial expressions used throughout the ages in different countries, all of which refer generally to falling 'insanely' in love or to being 'lovesick.'"[27]

In addition to lovesickness and OCD, high levels of serotonin in the brain have been linked to everything from depression to seasonal affective disorder to impulsive violence to rage. In fact, high serotonin levels coupled with surging levels of dopamine and the stress hormone cortisol may help explain the rage some lovers experience after they're dumped.

In her book *Why We Love,* anthropologist Helen Fisher explains the neurological basis for what forensic psychologist J. Reid Meloy calls abandonment rage: ". . . the basic brain network for rage is closely connected to centers in the prefrontal cortex that process reward-assessment and reward expectation. And when people and other animals begin to realize that an expected reward is in jeopardy, even unattainable, these centers in the prefrontal cortex

signal the amygdala and trigger rage . . . For example, when a cat's brain circuits for reward are artificially stimulated, they feel intense pleasure. If this stimulation is withdrawn, however, they bite. And each time the pleasure is withdrawn, the cat gets angrier."

Similarly, "hell hath no fury" like a woman or man scorned. Fisher tells the story of one of the subjects of her studies, Barbara. Barbara's brain had first been scanned for a study about people madly in love. At that time, she was glowing with health, optimism, and love for her partner, Michael. Five months later, when she had her brain scanned for a second time after Michael had rejected her, her colorless face was streaked with tears, she had lost weight, and she sadly described her misery: "I have a lump of unhappiness in my chest." Barbara's unhappiness turned to fury after she viewed a photo of Michael during her brain scan. She lashed out in anger at Fisher: "Why do you want to study this?"[28]

At the most extreme, some spurned lovers resort to stalking and violence—even murder. Most people, however, wallow in misery for a while and then slowly start to heal, especially if they meet another partner relatively quickly.

You might think one way of mitigating abandonment rage is to self-medicate—say, up your levels of serotonin. But as is the case with every love potion ingredient, it's not so simple and more isn't necessarily better. These chemicals work synergistically and can operate differently depending on which part of the brain and which part of the body are involved; also, picking one to elevate can backfire. For example, there are a number of well-documented side effects (including low libido) of widely prescribed antidepressants such as Prozac or

Paxil, known as selective serotonin reuptake inhibitors, which aim to increase serotonin levels.

Even the cuddle chemical oxytocin, which has potential as a treatment for autism and unassailable bonding credentials, also has a dark side according to recent research. Belgian researchers have found that oxytocin does not unconditionally promote trust—it makes people more cooperative when playing a social game if they've met their partners before the game, but makes them *less* cooperative when they play with an anonymous partner they know nothing about.[29] Dutch researchers have also found that their subjects become more ethnocentric under the influence of oxytocin. When asked to resolve a moral dilemma, such as choosing to save five lives from a runaway train by sacrificing one life, oxytocin-sniffing Dutch men more often saved fellow countrymen over Arabs and Germans than did the control group.[30] "It now seems clear that there's no free endocrine lunch. Even if oxytocin is just the thing to bring peace in our time to the rodents of the world, there's no single hormonal switch that can make us better humans," Robert M. Sapolsky, professor of neuroscience at Stanford University, wrote in an op-ed piece called "Peace, Love and Oxytocin" in the *Los Angeles Times*.[31]

A better strategy than trying to find a magic potion to enhance your life is to focus on your mind because your biochemistry matches your perceptions. Before I move on from love potions to the next chapter, which deals with the mind, this is a good time to point out that the cascade of chemicals that drive love can be unleashed not just by falling in love with a person but also by falling in love with a project or idea. Artists painting in a frenzy, entrepreneurs starting a business, a cell biologist writing about the Honeymoon Effect, a teenager in love—wherever there is passion, not far behind are the potent chemical brews that motivate us to pursue the objects of our desire.

CHAPTER 4

Four Minds Don't Think Alike

The magic of first love is
our ignorance that it can ever end.

—Benjamin Disraeli

You had the good vibes going. You were high from the love potions coursing through your body. You were humming all the crazy-in-love songs you've ever heard, and for once they made total sense. You had created the Honeymoon Effect with the love of your life, and you knew that this time it was going to last forever.

Except it didn't.

It all came crashing down, and you were left devastated and obsessed with what might have been. And puzzled: how could something so magical degenerate into endless, bickering recriminations and, if you were married, divorce court?

After all, you *wanted* it to work. You *believed* it would work. Maybe *The Biology of Belief* works for other people, you're thinking, but it doesn't for you. Yes, it does! But there's a catch, which explains why positive thinking and believing, by themselves, don't work.

The catch is that when you bonded so closely with your partner during those first blissful days and months, your behaviors and actions were controlled by the processing of your *conscious* minds. The conscious mind is the "creative" mind, the one that acts on behalf of your wishes and desires. So when the conscious minds of two lovers entangle, together they create magical harmony. Because honeymoon partners are operating from their deepest wishes and desires, the outcome of their interactions is . . . *voilà,* Heaven on Earth!

However, over time, your conscious mind becomes burdened with thoughts dealing with the busyness of everyday life—balancing your budget, scheduling your chores, planning your weekend. The processing of the *conscious* mind shifts from creating the honeymoon experience to the management and strategies needed to deal with perceived necessities. The result is that the *conscious* mind relinquishes behavioral control to default programs previously stored in the *subconscious* mind.

When it comes to partners, there are suddenly *four* instead of two minds involved. And these two "extra" subconscious minds can wreak havoc on Happily-Ever-After relationships. When our conscious minds stop paying attention to the moment, we lose control over our honeymoon creation because we unknowingly engage in preprogrammed behaviors we acquired through our developmental experiences. For many couples, once that subconscious programming comes to the fore, the honeymoon glow fades very quickly.

That's not surprising, because the behaviors programmed in the *subconscious* mind are primarily derived from observing and downloading *other* people's behaviors (many of them negative and disempowering) —especially those of your parents, immediate family, community, and culture. You start seeing a side of your partner (and yourself) that never emerged during the honeymoon. When the conscious mind stops paying attention to the current moment, you automatically and, most important, unconsciously engage in behaviors you downloaded from *others.*

Here's a scenario that may be all too familiar to you.

You're basking in the Honeymoon Effect, full of love for your supportive partner who lights up your life. Then one day you ask him a simple, loving question. He's not thinking about how good your relationship is. His *conscious* mind is preoccupied with fixing the car or paying the rent, so he responds reflexively and nastily with a tone that says, "Leave me alone." Shocked, you respond: "Who *are you?"*

You have just experienced the moment when honeymoons generally begin to fall apart. He responded so *unconsciously* that he didn't even notice how nasty he was. And, in his response to what he perceives as a personal "attack" on his character, he starts digging in his heels to defend himself to the death. He's thinking, *She accused me of not being me. I'm the same me I've always been. I don't know what she's talking about. What's her problem?*

Meanwhile, you're thinking, *Where is the loving man I married?* Your conscious mind detaches from the current moment to assess the unpleasant situation in which you now find yourself. Uh-oh, unbeknownst to you, you also unconsciously default to your own formerly hidden subconscious behaviors that you acquired from your family and culture. Now it's your partner's turn to be shocked as his once loving spouse shifts into criticism and blame, as well as other less than loving programs you downloaded from your parents.

As the daily issues of life increasingly occupy your and your partner's *conscious* minds, more disharmonious *unconscious* behavior patterns begin to rise to the surface. Soon you *both* shift from appreciating your partner to focusing on his or her periodic nasty outbursts. Both you and your partner turn defensive and begin to critique other faults: he never cleans up, she never puts the cap on the toothpaste, and on and on. All the things you ignored in the first glow of love now start to bug you.

If you met through an online dating service, both of you want your money back! *He/she didn't fill out the questionnaire honestly!* But actually you both filled it out in good faith. You both filled it out *consciously*—and that's the rub. Your thoughtful submissions from your conscious minds truly represent the people you aspire to be. Unfortunately, the character of the "you" who answered the questionnaire normally expresses itself only about 5 percent of the time. What both partners failed to include in their surveys were the sabotaging and limiting *subconscious* programs they acquired from others, which all of us unconsciously engage in about 95 percent of the time.

With the appearance of uninvited behaviors 95 percent of the time, you and your partner have most definitively left the honeymoon and are back on the road of conventional life. If any of these heretofore unseen, destructive, and disturbing behaviors had surfaced on the first day of your relationship, there probably would not have been a second day. Now you're wondering if you should lower your expectations and accept what your relationship has become, because "This is the way life is, and I have to accept the bad with the good." Or will the many compromises you make as you adjust to abusive behavior become so intolerable that your once seemingly unbreakable bond shatters? You say, "The hell with this. I can't do this." And then you go out (again) and try to find what you once had.

The culprit for this repeating cycle is invisible: it's the behaviors programmed in you and your partner's *subconscious* minds. Your conscious minds sent you on the quest to find a loving partner and rejoiced when you found the One, yet your subconscious mind is destroying what you've created. But once you know that you're dealing with *four* minds in the relationship, and once you know how to change the negative programming of your subconscious minds, you will have the tools to re-create what you've lost.

The High-Minded, Creative Conscious Mind

To better understand how this happens, let's talk more about the relationship between the brain and the mind. The human brain is a physical device like a radio. The mind, both conscious and subconscious, is analogous to the programming you hear on the radio. The activity of the conscious mind is primarily associated with the neural processing activity of the prefrontal cortex, the last evolutionary addition to the human brain.

The conscious mind is the seat of your personal identity. It identifies you as a distinct individual, a unique spirit. The conscious mind manages your personal wishes, desires, and aspirations. When I ask you what kind of relationships you want in your life, your lovely, high-minded answer comes from the conscious mind—I want a relationship based on love, equality, and respect as well as sexual chemistry. This is the "positive thinking" mind that optimistically sticks Post-it notes on the refrigerator that say, "I deserve a loving relationship" or "I eat healthy food."

This is also the creative mind that can look to the past and the future; it is not bound by time. Your conscious mind can answer questions about what you're doing *next* Wednesday or what you did *last* Wednesday. It's the mind that can "detach" from the current moment and daydream all day about what *might* happen—you might win the lottery. You might meet Prince Charming.

But wait a minute: if your conscious mind isn't paying attention and "managing" the present moment because it's busy thinking great thoughts or daydreaming about the kind of life you want to live, who is left to manage the "show"? Neuroscience researchers tell us that because of the conscious mind's ability to flit from thought to thought, humans, on average, use their personally creative *conscious* mind to control their behavior-regulating cognitive activity (as I mentioned on page 72, but it bears repeating) about 5 percent of the time. By default, the remaining 95 percent of

our cognitive activity is controlled by previously acquired programs downloaded into the *subconscious* mind.[1]

The Habitual, Record-Play Subconscious Mind

The subconscious mind is the mind that, Post-it notes be damned, compels us to lunge for the Krispy Kreme donuts in the refrigerator or fall for the biggest jerk at the party—again. The subconscious is associated with the neural activity of a much larger part of the brain (approximately 90 percent) than the conscious mind's prefrontal cortex. The subconscious mind is also a profoundly more powerful influence on our behavior than the conscious mind. The conscious mind's prefrontal cortex can process and manage a relatively measly 40 nerve impulses per second. In contrast, the 90 percent of the brain that constitutes the subconscious mind's platform can process 40 *million* nerve impulses per second. That makes the subconscious mind's processor *1 million* times more powerful than the conscious mind's.[2]

You might at this point be developing a decidedly negative attitude toward your powerful subconscious mind that is sabotaging your best efforts to create the Honeymoon Effect in your life—and to stay away from donuts. (Margaret refers to these as "circles of death.") But the subconscious mind plays a most important and valuable role in human development and in our daily lives. In any case, it's a waste of time to fight or blame the subconscious mind, as I'm tempted to do when I scarf down a Krispy Kreme donut. That's when my conscious mind berates me: *You stupid idiot. Why did you eat them when you just finished vowing to avoid them?*

I can yell all I want and blame all I want, but I'm wasting my time simply because there's nobody in the subconscious mind to respond to my rant! Demonizing your subconscious mind is akin to screaming at your television. Is your television good or bad? Neither. What are you *watching?* Don't blame the television set, blame the programming! Is your subconscious mind good or bad? Neither. The subconscious mind is primarily an amazing record/playback mechanism that, unlike the conscious mind, expresses little creativity and has no sense of time. It is always in the present moment, doesn't see a future, and certainly doesn't listen or care when you yell at it!

Rather than demonizing or battling with your subconscious over its bothersome behavioral programs, it's best to acknowledge its power. I grant you that this would be a very depressing book if I could only explain *how* your best intentions and your best love affairs have been sabotaged by your subconscious mind without pointing you to tools you can use to reprogram your subconscious mind. But thankfully, we are not doomed to live with our subconscious minds' self-sabotaging behaviors.

However, before I talk about how to reprogram your subconscious mind, I'll explain where all the negative programming came from (. . . not you). Then I'll point you to tools for reprogramming your subconscious mind so you can remove the invisible obstacles that are preventing you from creating and/or maintaining the Honeymoon Effect in your life.

Programming in Utero

Doctors used to think (and some still do) that all pregnant women can do to support their babies' health is eat well, take vitamins and minerals, and exercise; according to conventional thought, gene programs will manage the rest. But more recent research has laid to rest the myth that the unborn child is not sophisticated enough to react to anything other than its nutritional environment. It turns out that the more researchers learn, the more they realize how sophisticated the fetal and infant nervous system, which has vast sensory and learning capabilities, is. "The truth is, much of what we have traditionally believed about babies is false. We have misunderstood and underestimated their abilities. They are not simple beings but complex and ageless—small creatures with unexpectedly large thoughts," writes David Chamberlain in his book *The Mind of Your Newborn Baby.*[3]

In a world based on genetic control, where genes determine an organism's fate, science only needed to focus on the influence of the maternal blood's nutritional contribution in supporting fetal development. However, in the wake of the epigenetic revolution and new science revealing that environmental signals control gene expression, we now know that the developing fetus is influenced by more than just the nutrients in the mother's blood. Maternal blood also contains a vast array of "information" molecules, such as the chemicals, hormones, and growth factors that influence and control the mother's *emotional* and physical health.

Now we know that the very same chemicals that shape a mother's experiences and behaviors cross the placenta and target the same cells and genes in the fetus that they do in the mother. The consequence is that the developing fetus, bathed in the same blood chemistry as the mother, experiences the same emotions and physiology as the mother.

The fetus, for example, absorbs cortisol and other stress hormones if the mother is chronically anxious. If the child is unwanted for any reason, the fetus is bathed in the chemicals of rejection. If the mother is wildly in love with her baby and her partner, the fetus is bathed in the love potions you read about in the last chapter. If the mother is furious with the father, who has abandoned her during the pregnancy, the fetus is bathed in the chemicals of anger.

In my lectures I show a video from the Associazione Nazionale Educazione Prenatale because it graphically portrays the interdependent relationship between parents and their unborn child. In the video, a mother and father engage in a loud argument while the woman is undergoing a sonogram. You can see the fetus jump when the argument starts. When the argument escalates with the sound of shattering glass and even higher-pitched screaming, the fetus is fearful—it arches its body in a shock response and jumps higher, as if it were on a trampoline.

This sonogram and other research make it clear that fetuses react strongly to the environment provided by the mother and influenced by the father. Says Dr. Thomas R. Verny, whose pioneering 1981 book, *The Secret Life of the Unborn Child,* first laid out the case for the influence parents have even in the womb, "In fact, the great weight of the scientific evidence that has emerged over the last decade demands that we reevaluate the mental and emotional abilities of unborn children. Awake or asleep, the studies show, [unborn children] are constantly tuned in to their mother's every action, thought, and feeling. From the moment of conception, the experience in the womb shapes the brain and lays the groundwork for personality, emotional temperament, and the power of higher thought."[4]

The developing fetal brain not only responds to the chemical messengers in maternal blood; it also acquires a memory of these chemical cascades that define its in utero experiences. By the time a child is born, she or he has already downloaded the emotional "music" of behavior, a tune that will endure throughout the child's life. The child is born whistling a specific tune because he or she has already been programmed with the patterns of emotional chemicals experienced within the mother in the womb. It's not a single event like the argument I described that creates the programming—it's the repetitive patterns of the mother's emotional cascades. After birth, the child goes about the job of creating life experiences that become the lyrics that match the emotional music. That's great if the tune is a melody created in love, but it's not so great if the mother's emotional state was chronically unstable during her pregnancy.

The nature of this programming is important for adoptive parents whose children have come from chaotic backgrounds. These parents are often unaware that even when they adopted a child as an infant, their child may have already downloaded a pattern of dysfunctional emotional chemistry that becomes the "music" for a less than positive behavioral song—the child is not a blank slate. Adoptive parents shower attention on their children and are then shocked when the children they so lovingly nurtured start manifesting the behavior of their dysfunctional birth parents.

What they don't realize is that the foundation of a child's personality has already developed by the time of her or his birth. A new field of study known as fetal origins asserts that prenatal development constitutes the most consequential period of our lives, permanently influencing the wiring of the brain and shaping our intelligence and temperament. In her cover story for *Time* magazine, Annie Murphy Paul acknowledges, ". . . a pregnant woman's mental state can shape her offspring's psyche."[5] The nine months in the womb are so fundamental to human development in every area of life that Dr. Verny says he would like pregnant women to wear "Baby under Construction" T-shirts to broadcast this crucial fact. In truth, the mother (and by extension her relationship with the father) serves as nature's Head Start program. Through the mother's physiology, and especially her blood that crosses into the placenta, the fetus is indirectly learning about the world it will be born into and actively adjusting its behavior and genetics to survive in his or her parents' world.

Programming Post Utero

The pace of learning continues at warp speed after birth. Babies come into the world preprogrammed with some instinctual behaviors like suckling, but they have so much more to learn before they can navigate this world by themselves. No wonder evolution has endowed babies' and young children's brains with the ability to download an unimaginable number of behaviors and beliefs very quickly.

One key to understanding how this massive download takes place is the brain's fluctuating electrical activity as measured by EEGs. In adult brains, EEG activity ranges over five frequencies of brain waves, from the lowest-frequency delta waves to the highest-frequency gamma waves. But in young children the two lowest-frequency brain waves, theta and delta, predominate.[6a,b]

In the womb and through the first year of life, the human brain predominantly operates at the slowest brain-wave frequency, .5 to 4 cycles per second (Hz), known as delta waves. This isn't surprising because babies sleep a lot; in adults, delta waves predominate during our deepest sleep, when we dream and we're hardest to wake up.

From two to six years old, a child's predominant brain wave is theta (4 to 8 Hz), a vibrational frequency associated with the state of imagination. This is the stage of development when a child's delightful imagination runs wild. When you see a child with a broom and he or she says it's a horse, don't tell the child it's only a broom! It's a horse in the child's mind, because at this wonderful stage of life theta waves dominate brain function, a state in which imagination and reality become entangled. In the child's mind, the broom has become a horse.

Equally important, theta brain frequencies are associated with the state of hypnosis during which information can be directly downloaded into the subconscious mind. To induce this imaginative, suggestible state in adults, hypnotists use methods designed to drop their clients' brain-wave frequencies down into the mellower theta range.

For the first six years of life, children do not express the quality of consciousness associated with alpha, beta, and gamma EEG activity as predominant brain states. Children's brains primarily function below creative consciousness, just as adult brain activity drops below consciousness in sleep and during hypnosis. In their highly programmable theta state, children record vast amounts of information they need to survive in their environment, but they do not have the capacity to consciously evaluate the information while it is being downloaded. Anyone who doubts the sophistication of this downloading should think about the first time your child blurted out a curse word picked up from you. I'm sure you noted its sophistication, correct pronunciation, nuanced style, and context carrying *your* signature.

This ingeniously designed behavior-download system can be hijacked by hypercritical parents (and I'm not talking about the occasional swear word). Most of us grew up in families where we downloaded criticism from our parents: "You don't deserve that. You're not good at art. You're not smart. You're bad. You're a sickly child." Most often parents don't *mean* to say that their child is unlovable; they're acting like a coach who uses negative criticism to goad his players into trying harder.

Such parental coaching efforts require that children have the consciousness to interpret the positive logic behind their parents' negative critiques. But a child's brain predominantly operates below consciousness (alpha waves) in the first six to seven years of life. During those years, a child is unable to intellectually understand that verbal barbs are not true; the parent's negative assessments are downloaded as truth just as surely as bits and bytes are downloaded to the hard drive of your desktop computer. Critical parents have no idea that in their effort to help, they're actually sentencing their child to go through life feeling unworthy.

Here's an example: A dad is shopping at Kmart with his five-year-old son. The son spies a toy he becomes enthralled with and he has to have it *now*. When his dad says no, the child throws a huge tantrum that attracts the attention of every shopper in the toy section. Frustrated, the dad gets upset and angrily blurts out in his most authoritative, scary voice, "You don't deserve that!" The younger child directly downloads the dad's words and his rejecting tone at face value. I'm not good enough. I'm not lovable.

This "not lovable" programming is one of the biggest impediments to creating the Honeymoon Effect in your life. In fact, when subconscious programming is assessed with muscle testing, most people's subconscious minds reject the statement "I love myself."

I learned about the effectiveness of muscle testing the first time I went to a chiropractor after a serious motorcycle accident. The chiropractor demonstrated muscle testing as a means of communicating with the subconscious mind. He asked me to hold out my arm and resist the downward pressure he applied to it. I had no problem resisting the light force he put on my arm. Then he asked me to hold out my arm and resist him again, this time while saying, "My name is Bruce." Again, I had no trouble resisting his pressure.

Then he told me to hold out my arm and resist his pressure while saying, "My name is Mary." To my amazement, my arm flopped down, despite my strong resistance. "Try that again," I said. "Apparently, I wasn't ready." So we did, and this time I concentrated even more forcefully on resisting. Nevertheless, after I repeated, "My name is Mary," my arm sank like a stone. That's because when the conscious mind makes a statement that conflicts with a belief stored in the subconscious mind, the resulting disharmony is experienced as weakening of the body's muscles.

In my lectures, I often ask the audience to muscle test the phrase "I love myself." When the majority of arms sink, I ask them to think about how their subconscious belief that they are not lovable impacts their relationship. If you don't love yourself with both minds, what is the chance that other people will love you? Very low, because your subconscious mind does not believe you are lovable. If someone does claim they love you, how worthy can *they* be when even you don't find yourself lovable?

Subconscious programs of "unlovability," operating 95 percent of the time, unconsciously create behaviors that reveal how you feel. You may think it's a secret, deep thought, but it's playing all over your face in the words you unconsciously blurt out and the behaviors you display but don't observe. More important, your dysfunctional beliefs are broadcast in your energy field and can invisibly sabotage your efforts to create the kind of relationships your conscious mind so desperately seeks.

It's not only words that get lodged in people's subconscious minds during childhood programming but also behavior. In their theta-induced hypnagogic trance, children carefully *observe* as well as listen to their parents and then mimic their behavior by downloading it into their subconscious minds. When parents model great behavior, theta hypnosis represents a fabulous tool that enhances a child's ability to learn all kinds of skills to survive in the world. And when parental behavior is not so great, the same theta "recordings" can drag the child's life into the ground.

Research has shown that our close cousins, chimpanzees, share our ability to learn by observation alone. In a series of experiments over a period of two years at Kyoto University's Primate Research Institute, a female chimp was taught to identify the Japanese characters for a variety of colors. When the Japanese character for a specific color was flashed on a computer screen, the chimp learned to choose the right color swatch. Upon selecting the right color, she received a coin from the computer that she could then put in a vending machine to select a fruit treat.

Late in her training process, the chimp had a baby she held close to her through subsequent sessions. To the surprise of the researchers, one day, as the mother was retrieving her fruit from the vending machine, the infant chimp activated the computer. When the character appeared on the screen, the baby chimp selected the correct color, grabbed the reward coin, and then followed his mother to the vending machines. The astonished researchers were left to conclude that infants can pick up complex skills solely by observation and don't have to be actively coached by their parents.[7]

While this study and others have wonderful implications for learning, they have scary implications for children growing up in dysfunctional households with, for example, domestic violence or drug- or alcohol-addicted parents. They also have scary implications for less dramatically dysfunctional households. Just think about the information many of us downloaded about the unhealthy aspects of our parents' marriages! But, you say, "I'm different. I have vowed to create relationships that are *not* like the one my parents had." That's a laudable goal created by your *conscious* mind's wishes and desires, but meanwhile your dominant subconscious mind, programmed by your parents, is controlling your behavior.

Since it's sometimes hard to break through people's denial about their subconscious programming, think not about yourself but about a friend you've known for a long time—you know your friend "Bill" and you also know his dad. One day you recognize that Bill shares some of the same behaviors his dad expresses. Casually you offer, "Bill, you're just like your dad." That's when you had better back away from Bill! He goes ballistic and responds, "What do you mean I'm like my dad? I am *nothing* like my dad." The point of this story is that everyone else can see that Bill's behavior is like his dad's; it's only Bill who doesn't see his own subconscious programming!

And guess what: *"We are all Bill!"* We think we're acting out of the wishes, desires, and aspirations of our conscious mind. But as soon as our conscious mind starts to drift off in thought, it stops paying attention to the current moment. That's when the programs of our subconscious minds kick in. We start acting like our parents, and we don't even see it!

Now, you're wondering, when did the theta-induced download process stop? Around the age of six to seven, children become less susceptible to hypnotic programming as their developing brains start to function increasingly at higher-frequency alpha waves (8 to 12 Hz). Alpha wave activity is correlated with states of calm consciousness. Finally, the child begins to experience a sense of "self."

Let's revisit the Kmart scenario, but this time the child is ten years old and his brain is predominantly operating in conscious alpha-wave activity. This time when the child hears "You don't deserve that toy," he does not necessarily (except in abusive families) take his dad literally. He uses his conscious mind to evaluate the situation and tells himself this very accurate story: *My dad's angry because I'm slowing down the shopping—and he hates to shop! He wants me to shut up because he wants to finish shopping and go home and watch a football game. I know he loves me . . . and I* did *just get lots of new toys for my birthday last week . . .*

Of course, not all older children or adults are able to create such a perceptive accounting of their relationships. Even adults may fall into the same subconscious trap when they are not using their critical evaluating minds and they have a history of negative programming. But when children are very young they are incapable of creating such an assessment because, as I explained earlier, they are not operating from their conscious minds. In this anecdote, the five-year-old child's uncreative subconscious mind literally accepted his father's response as a statement of "truth." At ten, he can see the situation clearly for exactly what it is. But before he developed that conscious capability, he downloaded into his subconscious a lot of negative and disempowering information from both his parents and his community.

What does this have to do with the Honeymoon Effect? None of the programming you received before the age of six came from *your* wishes, desires, and aspirations. It came from observing your parents and your community, and that is the programming that primarily impacts how you approach relationships. It also explains the patterns of relationships: why some people look for love in all the wrong places, why some people can't sustain a relationship, and why some blessed people live a charmed life when it comes to relationships. For most people, who didn't have enlightened parents, this is the programming we need to undo before we can enjoy the Honeymoon Effect every day of our lives.

Reprogramming the Subconscious Mind

1. Be conscious of what you ask for

Over the years, Margaret and I have learned from personal experience a truth we have often heard before: to help yourself and to assist the Universe in helping you, it is important to visualize and list exactly what you want out of life. Wherever our goals are unclear, the Universe does its best to fill in the blanks. Unfortunately, it's what shows up in the details we did not plan on that can seriously undermine our desired goals and aspirations.

With that in mind, before you start reprogramming your subconscious mind, it would be best to step back and ask yourself *consciously:* "What is it that I really want?"

I used to tell people to be *careful* of stating what they want because they're going to get it, until my wonderful life partner, Margaret, pointed out how negative that admonition is. So I've changed the statement to one Margaret suggested: "Be *conscious* of what you ask for because you're going to get it."

Make a mental list of what you are looking for in a relationship. Fill in as many details as you can imagine, the more the better. This is an exercise that makes sure your conscious mind is creatively engaged in compiling the list. Details left out of your description, by default, will be determined by the subconscious mind, which if left to its own devices will list what your *parents* or your *community* believe would be a good relationship.

Write down the list in detail. As I said before, the more complete the details, the easier it is for your mind and the Universe to conspire in fulfilling your wishes and desires. Instead of "I want a great relationship," describe in multisensory detail what you want in the present tense as if you already have it. How does it look? How does it feel? What does it sound like? Here is one example, albeit a very incomplete one: "I love my caring, open-minded, affectionate, smart life partner, and I feel completely supported during our quiet evenings laughing and sharing our life stories and interests." By spelling out and broadcasting exactly what you want, you will manifest conscious and subconscious behaviors that will attract the kinds of relationships you want in your life.

2. Review your subconscious programming

While we focus on defining the characteristics of the mate we are seeking, we inevitably fail to assess whether our own behavior, especially the invisible, subconscious kind, would be compatible with the kind of partner we desire. For example, maybe you grew up in a family where your parents never expressed a loving relationship and were sharp with each other. You're determined to find a mate who will express those loving characteristics you didn't observe but now hunger for. Your conscious mind will generate behavior to attract your desired mate, but the predominant and unobserved subconscious behaviors you acquired from your parents may invisibly repel any contender who expresses these sought-after, loving traits.

We are mostly unaware of our own subconscious behaviors, and on the occasions we do notice them, it's almost shocking and embarrassing. As a result of not seeing our own behavior, we tend to blame others for our failed relationships: *How could someone as good as I am be the source of the problem?* True, in our conscious minds we are the loving people we think we are, but most of the time our lives are invisibly shaped by subconscious programs that may not be so lovable.

So we need to answer the question "Does my subconscious programming support my heart's desire?" If we are generally unobservant of these behaviors, how do we know what our programs are? Since most of the programming occurred before we were seven, and especially since much of our personality was defined before we were born, our conscious minds may have no clue what was downloaded into our subconscious minds. So how can we assess the character of our subconscious programming?

That is easy once you understand the interplay between the subconscious and conscious minds. Since 95 percent of our behavior is controlled by our subconscious autopilots, not our conscious minds, by definition our lives are physical printouts of the behaviors programmed in our subconscious minds.

If, for example, you've struggled with money all your life, think back, as a number of financial gurus now counsel, to the programming you received about money when you were young and how that programming is still impacting your life. In her book *The 9 Steps to Financial Freedom,* Suze Orman writes, "Messages about money are passed down from generation to generation, worn and chipped like the family dishes."[8] Orman, for example, learned very young that the reason her parents "seemed so unhappy" was not that they didn't love each other but that there was never enough money to pay the bills. "In our house money meant tension, worry, and sorrow."[9]

You can, as now wealthy Orman did, undo even the most negative programming. And you don't have to change your whole life! Just focus on the areas where you need help. Maybe money savvy comes naturally to you, but you struggle in relationships. No need to work on your subconscious programming regarding money. The things you like, the things that come easily to you, are already supported by positive subconscious programming—that's why you experience them. However, anything you have to work hard on, anything you've tried over and over to change with no success, anything you struggle to acquire—those are the areas that most likely represent limiting and self-sabotaging subconscious beliefs that need to be reprogrammed.

Not only do you not need to change everything, but it's not necessary to go to a psychologist to understand everything. You don't have to rip yourself apart emotionally. You don't have to focus on the people who are to "blame" for your programming. It's not necessary to kill the messenger. It's the message that needs to be rewritten because it's the message that has given rise to your behavior. So don't waste time going back and dwelling on the messenger, because that effort generally stimulates those old feelings that were so painful and brings them back to life again. All you have to do is focus on rewriting those subconscious behavioral programs that interfere with realizing your desires.

A note: Before you seek a loving relationship, make sure that this fundamental belief—"I love myself"—is lodged firmly in your subconscious mind. A lack of self-love, as I explained earlier, is a primary and huge obstacle for most people who want to create the Honeymoon Effect in their lives.

3. Start reprogramming

There are a number of techniques you can use to reprogram your subconscious mind. I'll tell you three categories of things I've done to undo my own negative programming (and there was plenty to undo) but do check the resources section in this book's appendix and at my website, www.brucelipton.com, so you can figure out which tools may work for you. There is no one-size-fits-all prescription. My goal is to present the information about the destructive role subconscious programming can play in your life and, I hope, to inspire you to find *the best way for you* to undo the programming.

Before we attempt to rewrite our behavioral programming, it is vitally important to understand the differing ways our conscious and subconscious minds learn. You might think that when the conscious mind learns something new, the subconscious program will automatically adjust itself to be in alignment with the new knowledge.

Wrong! The two minds essentially behave as separate entities and do not "learn" in the same way.

The creative, conscious mind, the "thinking" mind, can instantly learn from a variety of inputs. Something as simple as an "Aha" moment can produce a radical change in belief and in your life. Similarly, the conscious mind can acquire new beliefs from school and public lectures, reading self-help books, watching videos, or going through the excruciating psychoanalysis of your formative experiences. But sometimes seekers get stuck, as I did, by focusing on intellectual learning only. Educating the conscious mind does not automatically reprogram the subconscious mind. In my case, it was when I used the awareness I had acquired intellectually to rewrite subconscious programs that I made substantial progress in changing my life.

While the conscious mind is creative and can use that creativity to learn, the subconscious mind primarily learns through either hypnosis or the creation of habits. Before you were seven years old, your subconscious mind rapidly downloaded beliefs because your brain was predominantly operating in the hypnagogic theta EEG frequency. After age seven, the subconscious mind's primary source of learning is through habituation. How did you learn your multiplication tables? By repeating the sequence of numbers over and over, you eventually memorized the pattern and could repeat it unconsciously. Repetition leads to habituation, and that is the fundamental mechanism for programming subconscious behavior patterns.

When, for example, you were first learning to drive, your conscious mind was fully engaged with every detail, such as remaining aware of what you saw through the windshield, focusing on the dashboard gauges, keeping your eyes on the images in the three mirrors, and paying attention to your feet on the pedals. But today you get in the car, put the key into the ignition, and away you go, with your conscious mind focusing on your destination or the party you went to last night, or engaging in a deep conversation with a passenger. Most of the time you are not even paying conscious attention to what's happening on the road. Who's driving the car? The subconscious mind, using the habits it acquired through the repetitive periods of practice when you were learning how to drive. Don't be afraid of the thought that you are not consciously driving the car because, as I mentioned earlier in the chapter, the subconscious mind is a million times more powerful and has a significantly faster processor than the conscious mind. In fact, if your car starts to skid off toward an accident, stress hormones will shut down your conscious processing to ensure that the faster and more powerful subconscious controls the situation.

Hypnosis and habituation are the primary means of programming behavior into the subconscious mind. That is why conscious mind efforts, such as giving yourself a "good talking to," reading a self-help book, or posting sticky notes have little influence on changing undesired subconscious programs unless they are regularly repeated so as to create a new habit.

a. Mindfulness/Habit: The first thing I did when I became aware that I needed to rewrite my programming was to create the habit of mindfulness—I started by paying attention to my thoughts! The goal of mindfulness is to make your every action and decision come from your wishes and desires; i.e., your *conscious* mind, not your autopilot, subconscious mind.

What I learned when I started paying attention was not only how often I slipped into automatic pilot while my conscious mind drifted off in thought, but how often those autopilot thoughts were not helpful. Researchers have corroborated that 65 percent of our thoughts are negative and/or redundant.[10]

One way to start this practice is to observe your thoughts when you're doing a mundane chore such as driving. When you're stopped at a stoplight, you'll quickly learn that stopped traffic is not dead time—thoughts are continuously running through your head. When I started observing these runaway thoughts, I realized that they were not describing a reality I wanted to live in, yet they were what I was manifesting. (Sample: *I'll never get there on time. I don't want to do this. This traffic is a nightmare.*) As I've explained, positive thoughts aren't enough, but they're a good start. So with intention, I began to immediately rewrite negative thoughts as they popped into my mind, giving them a positive spin while simultaneously making an effort to *consciously* stay in the moment. Repeatedly rewriting a frequent and particular thought will generate a habit that will automatically "correct" the negative thought before it even comes into consciousness.

Mindfulness is very difficult to maintain when life gets busy because our thoughts are continuously flitting about and managing the innumerable details of everyday life. This interfering busyness is why Buddhist mindfulness is a lifelong practice.

In 2010 researchers at Harvard University found that people spend almost half their waking hours thinking about something other than what they're doing and that this mind-wandering makes them unhappy (even when their minds wander to pleasant subjects). The authors wrote, "In conclusion, a human mind is a wandering mind, and a wandering mind is an unhappy mind. The ability to think about what is not happening is a cognitive achievement that comes at an emotional cost."[11] Mind-wandering unhappiness, of course, is exacerbated by the fact that while our minds are wandering, our invisible subconscious programs are often sabotaging our life's desires.

For this book, the most significant finding of the Harvard study is that mindfulness is a lot easier when you're making love. The study found that mind-wandering occurred on average only 10 percent of the time when the subjects were having sex.[12] This explains why honeymooners have an easier time operating *consciously*. When we stay mindful—not just when we're having sex—the wishes and desires of our *conscious* minds will manifest in our lives, which is how we can make sure the Honeymoon Effect lasts!

b) Hypnosis/Subliminal Tapes: When we awaken from deep sleep, the brain's frequency vibrations jump from the slow, unconscious delta waves to higher frequency theta. This is the brain state associated with imagination, as I've described. It is also associated with a state of twilight reverie in which one seamlessly blends the real and dream worlds together. A theta-driven experience blends imagination and reality, a behavioral characteristic best seen in children younger than seven years of age. As an adult, you may have experienced a theta moment when a clock radio woke you. In your groggy state you mixed a real story on the radio with a dream you were waking up from. This is an example of how you can blend imagination with reality.

As you become more awake, brain EEG activity ramps up to higher-frequency alpha waves, whose character of calm consciousness fills your head. By the time you get to work, your brain is in work mode operating with high-speed, high-functioning beta waves. Hopefully, when you return home from the job, the frequency of your EEG waves drops off sequentially as the brain slows down from beta to calming alpha and then drifts off into theta and finally into delta, fast asleep.

This ramping up and down of EEG frequencies means that twice a day your brain passes through the programmable hypnagogic theta phase. So every day you have two opportunities to reprogram subconscious beliefs through a natural state of hypnosis. Of course, as a number of studies have found, meditators can increase the frequency of theta waves. For example, a 2009 study of experienced practitioners of Acem Meditation, a nondirective method developed in Norway, were asked to rest for 20 minutes and to meditate for another 20 minutes. During meditation, "significantly increased theta power" was found, especially in the frontal and middle parts of the brain.[13]

Once I became aware that children download vast amounts of information in their hypnagogic state, I decided to try this myself by using subliminal tapes designed to program positive thoughts and beliefs into my subconscious mind. I picked up a Louise Hay (the Grand

Dame of self-empowerment, and coincidentally, the publisher of this book) tape to reduce stress and enhance patience. The tape opened with a relaxation exercise designed to calm down the conscious mind and move the listener into the relaxed, programmable state attributed to the low-frequency alpha and theta brain waves.

The first time I put on headphones and activated the subliminal tape as I was going to sleep, my conscious mind stayed alert the whole time and heard the tape's programming message repeated a number of times. By the third time I used the tape, I never even made it through the relaxation exercises before I fell asleep. It got to the point that as soon as I put on the earphones, I instantly relaxed. The neat thing is that the tape was continuously downloading positive thoughts while I was drifting into the low-frequency brain waves of a child. It was effortless. I just had to put on the earphones and I would fall asleep.

The changes I experienced were subtle—they didn't stand out like a neon sign. But things were not exactly the same as they had been. They were better. It was only after a period of time, when I looked back and reviewed the events in my recent life, that I realized how profoundly my behavior had changed.

c) Energy Psychology: The next step I took for reprogramming my subconscious was to utilize a new method of healing called energy psychology. As you'll see in the list of energy psychology resources in the appendix and on my website, there are many different versions of energy psychology. In spite of the wide variations in practice among the different modalities, one thing is clear. Energy psychology can induce radical changes in behavior within minutes and in many cases, these changes produce permanent alterations in subconsciously programmed behaviors.

I love these new technologies because they completely undermine the prevailing (and behavior-controlling) belief that change is hard or difficult. I clearly see that statement now as just another disempowering belief that encourages resistance to change. It's also wonderful that these new psychology tools are available to us at a point in time when evolution is pushing humanity to make changes *now*. Necessity is the mother of invention. We don't have years and years to change human behavior.

While no mechanism has been identified to account for the rapidity of behavioral changes that result from these practices, the fact is that the changes are real and long lasting. Personally, I am most familiar with the PSYCH-K belief change process developed by Rob Williams. I know PSYCH-K's energy-balancing technology is effective because it radically changed my life. More important, over the last few years I have heard from hundreds of people around the world who have used PSYCH-K to successfully take charge of their lives.

Until recently, the feel-good results of energy-balancing technologies were simply subjective experiences of individuals. However, new 3-D brain-mapping studies employing quantitative electroencephalography (QEEG) and low resolution electromagnetic tomography (LORETA) have provided measurable, objective data that reveal significant and lasting changes in brain behavior following a single ten-minute PSYCH-K session.[14]

Brain-mapping studies reveal that PSYCH-K induces a "whole-brain state," wherein both right and left cerebral hemispheres begin to work together, a functional situation known as hemispheric synchronization. In our normal wakeful condition, we tend to operate predominantly from our left hemisphere, the side of the brain preoccupied with logic. In contrast, the right hemisphere is associated with processing emotions. When the left hemisphere is dominant, we tend to overrule our emotional drives with logic and reason.

According to neuroscientist Jeffrey L. Fannin, Ph.D., whole-brain activity positively affects more than just physical and psychological healing. Dr. Fannin's brain-mapping research indicates that whole-brain function is a "gateway to higher consciousness," tantamount to a state of superlearning associated with higher functionality and spiritual consciousness.[15] Please understand that the PSYCH-K process does not work for everybody. In truth, there is no one tool that fits all people. If one of the processes listed in the appendix doesn't work, don't give up; try another one!

4. Communication

To create the Honeymoon Effect, it is imperative that couples learn to communicate on a deep level, and that kind of communication can't happen if both people don't have the same level of awareness. When both partners are aware of the subconscious roadblocks they face, they can focus on turning what would normally be arguments into discussions. "I don't think you heard what you just said. Did you mean that? Is that a tape you're playing? Is that a behavior you downloaded from your father?" All of these discussion points offer an opportunity for both partners to become aware of their unconscious behaviors while gaining an understanding of how their subconscious behavioral programs can undermine a relationship.

If only one person in the couple is aware of this behavioral programming, trying to engage in change would be like talking to a brick wall. If one person is not interested in or ready for change, then change simply will not occur. Change requires a team effort!

5. Patience

If you come to a trouble point in your relationship one week and that same trouble point pops up again the week after, don't be surprised. Remember, you are trying to change lifelong patterns; change in relationships may not occur overnight. To break recurring dysfunctional patterns, you need to have patience with yourself, with each other, and with the stubborn habits that continue to rear their ugly heads. If you can deal with the issues in terms of a discussion instead of an argument, you are already on the path to a new life.

For example, here's a prototypical issue. The boy gets into a dispute with the girl and doesn't want to talk about it. The girl, on the other hand, wants to dissect it. That could be a recipe for disaster as she keeps talking and he keeps digging a deeper hole in his silence. In my case, when I finally came out of that hole, I owned that my noncommunication "habit" was delaying resolution of our issues and realized that Margaret was earnestly trying to repair the potholes that were showing up in our lives.

Later, when I found myself in a calm, cool place, I told Margaret that while I was in the midst of that habitual disconnect process, I was still listening, even though I couldn't yet engage. I asked her to be patient with me. I told her I wanted her to keep talking while I internally tried to escape from my destructive habitual behavior. After that moment of deep insight and awareness, each subsequent time I responded by disconnecting, my conscious mind more effectively took control and terminated that dysfunctional behavior. Over a short time, repetition rewrote that limiting behavior, and we now easily resolve issues without invoking unconscious, knee-jerk responses. No more confrontations . . . boy, is life easier. *Yea!*

6. Practice

How many times did you practice your multiplication tables until they stuck? How many times did you practice driving before you became adept? Similarly, subconscious habits don't go away just because you say, "Go away." You have to practice your new habits until they become automatic. A habit is not just words emblazoned on a refrigerator Post-it note. A habit is behavior you practice until it sticks!

Eventually, the tools I described will bring about the changes you seek. I'm a scientist, and my relationship with my partner, Margaret, who has taught me so much, is an ongoing experiment in living Happily Ever After for both of us. I can tell you for sure that I wouldn't be writing this book if the experiment wasn't working!

When you remove the impediment of your subconscious programming, you are free to live a life that is a creative romance, a dream come true. Once you program your conscious mind's wishes, desires, and aspirations into your subconscious mind, you will create a perpetual honeymoon. Even when you shift into automatic pilot, as we all do, formerly ugly behaviors will simply not rear their heads because your subconscious programs will now match the desires and wishes in your conscious mind. When all four of your minds are aligned, you and your partner will become the same lovable people you were in the first days of your relationship.

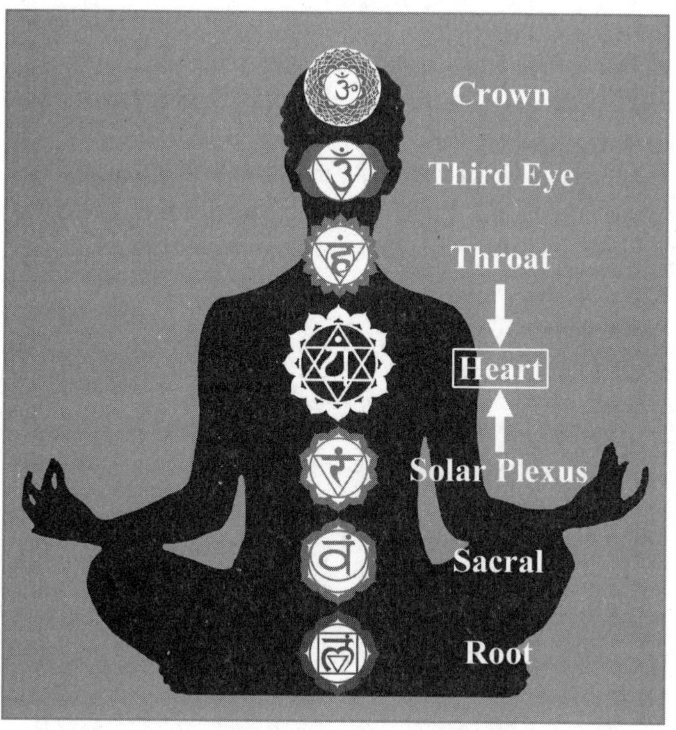

The above illustration of the seven main chakras, energy points that run up and down the body, visually illustrates the romantic consequence of uniting your physiology and behavior. In this chart, the three lower chakras (the solar plexus, sacral, and root) represent the influence of our physical biology, specifically our physiology, in shaping our lives. The top three chakras (the crown, third eye, and throat) represent the influences derived from our consciousness, our psychology. The middle chakra is the heart chakra, which represents unconditional love for self and others.

When all seven of the chakras in this illustration are aligned, there are no energy blocks; energy flows freely through every chakra. The heart chakra in the middle is purposefully larger than the others because when you align your physiology and your psychology, when you love yourself so others can love you and you can love others, your heart will expand and open to your partner and to the world. By manifesting the life you *choose,* not the life you were programmed by your family to lead, you can have it all.

Welcome to the Honeymoon Effect!

CHAPTER 5

Noble Gases: Spreading Peace, Love, and Tulsi Tea

Be the change that you wish to see in the world.

—Mahatma Gandhi

I hope I've convinced you in the previous chapters that you can create the relationships of your dreams. In this chapter I'd like to convince you that the Honeymoon Effect is about more than two people creating a wonderful relationship—it's about "noble gases" spreading the healing glow of love around this ailing planet.

Noble Gases

To explain that sweeping statement, I need to go back to chemistry. Not to the chemical stew of love potions that course through your body when you're madly in love (Chapter 3) but to the elements in the periodic table that either vexed or entranced you when you studied chemistry in high school. You won't be surprised to learn that I was entranced (English class was another matter) and still am by the insight into the nature of the Universe that the ordered pattern of the 118 elements in the periodic table revealed.

The periodic table is a masterpiece of organized chemical information that defines the traits and characteristics of the physical universe. I am especially intrigued by the unique characteristics of the six noble gases, the elements comprising the last column on the right of the table, a subdivision identified as "Group 18." Noble gas elements include helium (He); neon (Ne); argon (Ar); krypton (Kr) . . . no, this is not the element that zapped Superman's strength; xenon (Xe); and radon (Rn). The most significant aspect of these odorless and colorless gases is that noble gases are the only elements in the periodic table that don't (except under very special circumstances) form chemical compounds.

The other 112 elements in the periodic table readily form chemical bonds with one another to create the physical molecules that make up the stars, the planets, and the biosphere. The secret to why atoms create "chemistry"—specifically, why atoms naturally tend to bond with one another—can be explained by comparing the structures of the noble gas atoms with the other elements in the periodic table.

In the structure of an atom, the protons have positive charges and the electrons have an equal, but opposite, negative charge. The number of positive protons in an atom is equal to the number of its negative electrons; hence, every atom is electromagnetically neutral with no net charge. The magic of the chemistry that creates the Universe is not based on the number of charged particles in an atom but on their distribution. While protons are massed together in the atom's nucleus, electrons orbit around the nucleus like satellites.

In the simplest description, orbiting electrons are distributed in concentric layers (shells) around the central nucleus. Each shell can only contain a specific number of electrons (shell 1 = 2 electrons, shell 2 = 8 electrons, shell 3 = 18 electrons, shell 4 = 32 electrons, and shell 5 = 50 electrons). With the exception of the first shell, the shells are made up of several subshells. When a particular shell or subshell is filled with its maximum number of electrons, additional electrons are then distributed to the next outer concentric shell. If that layer becomes filled, the extra electrons are added to the next outer shell, and so on.

Now here's the catch: atoms spin like nanosize tornados. When a shell is not completely filled with its maximum number of electrons, it causes the atom to wobble as it spins. Consider this simple analogy: the drum of a washing machine spins like an atom. What happens if you place a bunched-up blanket on one side of the drum and start up the machine? As the machine spins, the washer begins to wobble and bounce around, creating quite a ruckus. An unfilled electron shell in a spinning atom results in similar wobbly behavior at the nano level.

In our laundry analogy, to stop the racket you open the lid of the washing machine and redistribute the blanket evenly around the drum. Now when you restart the machine, it spins in perfect, peaceful balance. The 112 different elements whose electron shells are incomplete seek to balance their wobble by bonding with other atoms that have a complementary wobble. When bonded together, the two imbalanced atoms spin in harmony.

The number of shells occupied by electrons and the status of the outer shell's fulfillment define an atom's chemical activity. Noble gases are unique elements because they are the only ones that naturally possess filled outer shells. Because they already spin in perfect balance, noble gases do not normally seek partnership with other elements and are therefore chemically inactive.

In contrast, the chemical bonding among the other 112 elements represents the effort of wobbly atoms to generate spin-balance. Thus chemical bonding is a codependent relationship; in such pairings, each atom depends upon—"needs"—another atom to acquire peace and harmony. The key word in describing these relationships is need.

Let's consider the character of a sodium and chlorine atom, elements that are a perfect match for each other. Chlorine (Cl) has a total of 17 electrons that occupy three shells: two electrons in its first shell (maximum capacity), eight in its second shell (maximum capacity), and seven in its outermost shell. To acquire spin-balance, chlorine would need one more electron to fill a space in its outer shell (see Arrow B in the following illustration).

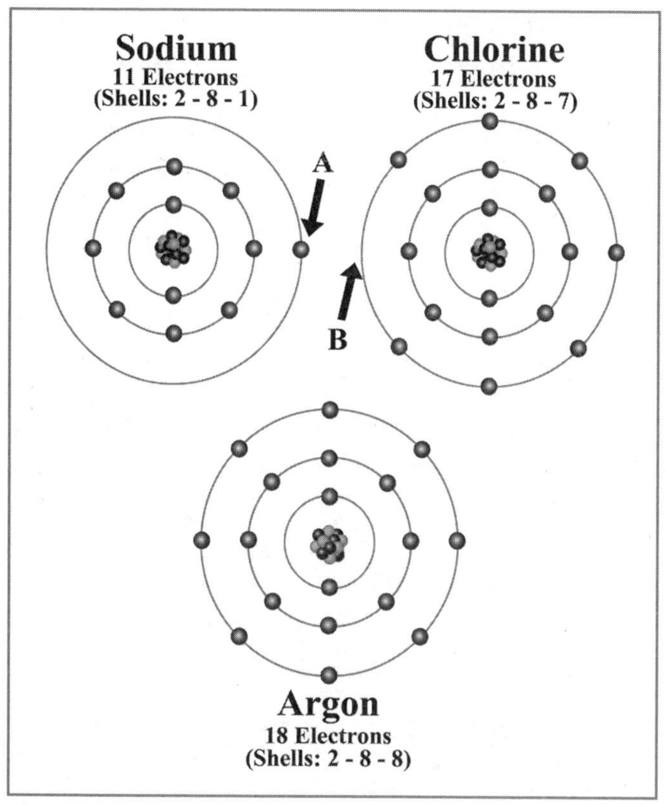

A simplified illustration of a sodium, a chlorine, and an argon atom. The atom's central nucleus is a cluster of positively charged protons and uncharged neutrons. Surrounding the nucleus are electrons distributed in rings that represent the atom's shells. Argon atoms spin in balance because their outer shells are filled with the full complement of electrons. In contrast, sodium and chlorine atoms spin with a wobble because their outer electron shells are incomplete.

In contrast, sodium (Na) has 11 total electrons in its three shells: two in its first shell (maximum capacity), eight in its second shell (maximum capacity), and only one electron in its outer shell. To acquire spin-balance, sodium's outer shell would either need to add seven more electrons or lose its solitary electron (Arrow A in illustration on the previous page).

Neither sodium's nor chlorine's outer electron shell is complete. Separately their spin behavior resembles the wobble produced by the imbalanced blanket in a washing machine. But when sodium and chlorine atoms get together, they "make chemistry." They fulfill this Universe's tendency to find balance by combining—they lose their wobble and stabilize. By creating what is referred to as an ionic bond, sodium loans its single outer shell electron to its chlorine partner, which uses the extra electron to complete its outer shell (see the arrow in the figure below). *Voilà!* Through their pairing, each atom now has a complete outer shell, and together they spin in perfect balance. This is a relationship based upon fulfilling each other's needs.

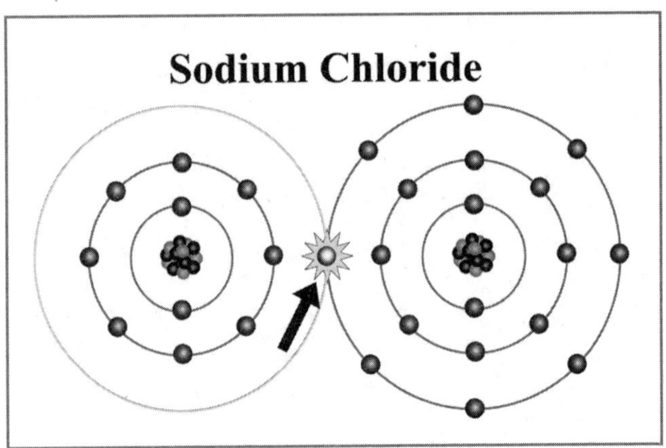

As I explained in the last chapter, because of conventional familial and cultural parenting practices that are less than optimal, almost all of us are, to a certain degree, psychologically "unbalanced." As imbalanced individuals, we have a tendency to do the same thing that atoms do—we seek a complementary partner who is out of balance as well. When two partners complement each other's imbalances, together they can spin "harmoniously" with no wobbles.

While our conscious minds seek partnership with individuals who fulfill our wishes and desires, our subconscious minds are unconsciously seeking individuals who possess traits that complement our personal, but unobserved, imbalances. In an example of an extreme codependent relationship, sadists who love to inflict pain seek pair bonding with masochists who derive pleasure from receiving pain.

In the unconscious process of creating codependent relationships, you won't lose any electrons, but you may think you're losing your mind living with the imbalanced partner your *subconscious mind* attracted, not the wonderful partner your conscious mind envisioned. But even when your posthoneymoon relationship deteriorates and the partner of your nightmares starts to pull away, you may not want to let him or her go! You may find yourself screaming, "Don't *leave* me!" You know your partner is abusive, but you don't want to let him go because he provides balance, albeit a dysfunctional balance, in your life. And that is the definition of codependency!

Remember the woman in the Caribbean I drove crazy because I wouldn't argue with her? You can imagine the kind of programming she received as a child that led her to link love with abuse and screaming. People will seek whatever they recognize as love, even a perverse form of love, because, as I explained in Chapter 1, there is a biological drive for coupling and a biological/psychological drive to gravitate toward what you consider love. To feel balanced, she *needed* someone to fight with! Even though she complained about her former partner, she didn't want to change; she unconsciously sought more abuse. And one thing I've learned in my life is that you can't change another person: unless someone *asks* for your help, your efforts are likely doomed.

Of course, as I've made clear in this book, I was no paragon of balance either. Remember the woman in the Caribbean who correctly told me I was too needy? I was desperate to fulfill my biological imperative to couple and find balance, but I was looking for love in all the wrong places. Actually, like the woman who equated love with screaming, I was looking for love in exactly the "right" places given how cluttered my subconscious mind was with negative programming. I was unconsciously looking for a codependent relationship to balance my life.

Noble Gases: Lasers and Love

Now let's look at the chemical equivalent of the better way I described in the last chapter. Once you've aligned your conscious and subconscious minds, you are no longer a sodium atom desperately looking for a chlorine atom; you become a noble gas spinning in perfect balance—you don't "need" another element to be balanced.

You might think that makes noble gases strange elements to use as inspirational models for this last chapter of *The Honeymoon Effect,* and I grant you that at first glance, noble gases sound more like Ayn Rand than Rumi! Poor argon, poor neon, etc.—they're never going to experience true love because they spin so well on their own that they'll never need a partner!

It is true that when people spinning in balance like a noble gas have the opportunity to jump into another dysfunctional relationship, they do not seize it. Wobbly atoms around them can act as crazy as they want, but noble gases are not drawn in; instead, they keep spinning happily on their own. As I tell my audiences, "Noble gases can love the jerk, but they are not *attached* to the jerk!"

It is also true that noble gases can live perfectly happily on their own. When I rewrote my negative subconscious programming (vestiges still pop up from time to time), I came to peace within myself—I was finally able to pass the "I am lovable" test, and, for the first time, I didn't *crave* a partner to make me feel whole. In fact, for a long while I didn't have a partner and wasn't missing one; I was living a life of passion, spreading the word of the new science that genes do not determine our lives or our relationships. I had become passionate about connecting with like-minded new friends—I was flying solo yet experiencing the Honeymoon Effect in my life.

But, you persist, how can noble gases fare in relationships given their propensity to spin so well on their own? The answer is, "Spectacularly!"

To understand that surprising answer, we must consider another characteristic of noble gases, their ability to form *excimers*. An excimer, short for "excited dimer," is a special bonding association between two atoms that would not be bound together in their normal state. When a noble gas atom is hit by a photon of light, its "normal" state is profoundly altered. The atom absorbs the photon's energy and begins to vibrate faster because of its higher level of energy. Simply, an "enlightened" noble gas atom becomes "excited." A noble gas atom in an excited state *will* seek bonding, partnership with another noble gas atom so it can share that excitement! Excited noble gas atoms form excited dimers (excimers) that are chemically represented as: Ar_2, Kr_2, Xe_2, He_2, Ne_2, and Rn_2.

Unlike conventional "chemistry," which is based on codependent bonding to produce spin-balance and stability, energized noble gas atoms are like people primed and ready for selfless love, a world of sharing and caring. By reworking my imbalanced subconscious programs, I believe I had become an "excited boy" spinning in balance when Margaret eventually appeared in my life and we created our still enduring Happily Ever After excimer (see Epilogue).

I'm reminded of the documentary movie *After Happily Ever After,* a whimsically entertaining look (complete with a Las Vegas Elvis impersonator) at marriage in the United States, where 90 percent of us marry but only 50 percent of our marriages last. In that movie, Stephanie Coontz, author of *Marriage, a History: How Love Conquered Marriage,* says, "This is the first time ever in thousands of years when marriage has been not only about love but also about mutual respect and equal options of men and women . . . When a marriage works, it's fairer, more fulfilling, more protective of its members (both adults and children) than ever before in history." That sounds like a definition of marriage between noble gases to me!

The excited relationship of an excimer results in its emitting extra energy as another photon of light.

Excimer couples glow! Under normal circumstances, the life span of a glowing, solitary excimer is rather short. However, if there are other noble gas atoms in the vicinity, they can absorb that emitted photon and become excited themselves, which means excimers can lead to the creation of more excimers. This excitable characteristic of noble gases led to the development of the laser, which is an acronym for Light Amplification by Stimulated Emission of Radiation.

A laser is a tube filled with noble gas atoms that are then excited by energy. The energy stimulates the formation of excited noble gas dimers (partnerships). The activated excimers then radiate and emit their own photons, which in turn activate other noble gas atoms in the community to form excited dimers. As the population of activated excimers increases, their emitted photons ultimately create a chain reaction that results in "light amplification" through the production of more and more radiating excimers. Only a dim glow of light is produced at first. However, as the stimulated emission of excimer radiation increases, the light gets brighter and brighter. Creating coherence among the emitted photons by aligning their light waves so that they are all in phase results in the production of a laser beam, a stream of light so powerful it can burn a hole through a steel wall.

I once produced a laser light show, and I can tell you from personal experience that the kaleidoscopic colors, intensity, and purity of laser light have a powerful, mesmerizing impact on audiences. "Enlightened" noble gas–like humans can make a similarly powerful impact on our planet, because they understand the truth of entrepreneur, humanitarian, and philanthropist Bharat Mitra's words: "Alive in each person's heart is the desire to participate in something bigger than themselves." They gravitate to other noble gases as Bharat Mitra (Yoav Lev) and his wife Bhavani (Holly B.) Lev (founders of ORGANIC INDIA) did when they created a community that is helping to heal our planet (more on this later).

It doesn't take a rocket scientist, a climate scientist, an antiwar activist, or a cell biologist to figure out that this planet needs healing. There's a name for what humanity is experiencing right now. When the cells in our bodies fight one another, we call that autoimmune disease. What humanity, the superorganism comprising seven billion people on this planet, is experiencing now is a very bad case of autoimmune disease.

With the exception of human beings, all organisms that make up the biosphere are in cooperation with one another. We, on the other hand, are creating our own extinction because of our disconnection from nature. Projections that there will be no fish left in the ocean in 30 years sound like a science fiction nightmare, but they are a scientific reality and one warning among many that we have to change the way we live. Whether it's disease or social crises, all of the troubles humanity is facing stem from our inability to understand that when we destroy the environment we are destroying ourselves. Just as James Lovelock's Gaia theory posits, our planet is an integrated and complex superorganism; we are an integral part of this environment, and when we destroy the environment we are destroying ourselves.[1]

If Mother Nature were to put human civilization on trial for perpetrating this planet-destroying, dangerous autoimmune disease, a defense team emphasizing the Darwinian belief in the survival of the fittest would likely point to stellar human beings like Einstein and Beethoven to argue that humans do not deserve to be condemned. This argument wouldn't get very far, for evolution isn't about the fittest *individuals* in a species; it's about the impact of the species as a whole. In this case, the collective actions of the seven billion people on this planet have created a track record that is abysmal and indefensible.

Humanity's options are clear: we can continue to do what we're doing and go the way of the dinosaurs, or we can change our way of life. Despite our penchant for destruction, I am an optimist. Evolution, as I explained in Chapter 1, is powered by the formation of cooperative communities, and I believe today's chaos will push us (some kicking and screaming) to the next stage of evolution where loving, cooperative noble gases thrive.

However, we can't just sit in an easy chair and then one day get up and open the door to greet the new world. Evolution is an active process not a passive one, and every one of us has to be a participant. I subscribe not only to Lovelock's Gaia theory but also to his wise advice about avoiding "us versus them" thinking:

> If we are all to live well with the Earth and survive this century, we have to understand that to strive for human rights alone is not enough. We have to understand that we and all living things from bacteria to trees, from amoeba to whales are all part of this great living Earth System. Most important, we have to act personally and not expect others to do our duty . . . We tend far too much to seek scapegoats, people to blame for the environmental troubles, whereas it is us all. We determine everything we do and we've got to keep that in mind.[2]

I grant you that it's difficult to follow Lovelock's advice when reading depressing headlines about oil spills and corrupt business and political leaders. I find it a lot easier to avoid scapegoating when I focus on noble gases doing their part to change the world. That's why I decided to end this chapter by introducing you to a few of the noble gases I've had the privilege of connecting with on my long and fascinating journey from agnostic scientist to spiritual scientist.

Roses, Tulsi, and Dignity

When Margaret and I received an invitation to travel to India to meet Bharat Mitra and Bhavani Lev, we felt compelled to go. How could we resist meeting in person (not just on Skype) a couple who had founded a loving community and company called ORGANIC INDIA, whose philosophy embraces Gaia: "Creation is one. The Earth is one. We are one."

Like many Westerners, Bharat Mitra (from Israel) and Bhavani (from the United States) went to India as spiritual seekers. In India, they found a guru, Sri H. W. L. Poonja (Papaji), and a simpler life. But unlike most pilgrims, they stayed in India to make Lucknow (the capital of the state of Uttar Pradesh and where they lived with Papaji) their home and the headquarters of ORGANIC INDIA. Says Bhavani, "We felt called to start an organic revolution in India." Acting as enlightened noble gas excimers, Bharat Mitra and Bhavani excited other "noble-gas" participants to create a community to share their light, not only among themselves but with the rest of the world as well.

They started their revolution in 1997 in the town of Azamgarh. In the '60s, many farmers in this community had embraced the high-tech "Green Revolution" farming methods that Western corporations had introduced to India. They mortgaged their farms and lives to buy the promise of costly genetically modified seeds; and then had to borrow more to pay for the synthetic fertilizers, pesticides, and modern irrigation projects required to grow the genetically modified plants. The goal was to fend off the country's famines that had once been considered inevitable, and at first it seemed to work. Yields increased and formerly poverty-stricken towns and the farmers who lived in them prospered.

But by the time ORGANIC INDIA started its work in Azamgarh, many farmers had become disillusioned and desperate. Their fields had indeed turned green but in the process had sucked up so much groundwater that they needed to dig deeper and deeper wells and borrow more and more money. The genetically modified organisms (GMOs) and petrochemical sprays produced an environmental disaster with devastating consequences. Monsanto's GMO "monster crops" accelerated depletion of soil nutrients, creating plant blight, which in turn led to an invasion of destructive insects. The farmers had to borrow more money to buy more and more chemicals to grow their crops to fend off pests that had become resistant. In the last decade, nearly 200,000 Indian farmers, unable to continue to work their depleted land and unable to make loan payments, took their own lives—many by drinking the very pesticides they had been told would ensure a good livelihood for them and their families.[3]

Unsurprisingly, when ORGANIC INDIA arrived in Azamgarh, farmers were suspicious of more Westerners asking them to radically change the way they work. And just as a practical matter, they were leery of becoming organic farmers, because it takes at least three years to certify a field as organic.

Despite these suspicions, one farmer named Kailash Nath Singh decided to take a chance by going organic on his small, three-acre farm. That small step couldn't have been more symbolic; not only was Singh going back to the way his ancestors had farmed but he was doing it with the ancient crop tulsi (also called holy basil), a wild medicinal herb that has been used for thousands of years in traditional Indian medicine (Ayurveda) to heal body and mind.

Now, thanks to ORGANIC INDIA's subsidies during their transition, 15 years later there are 1,000 organic farmers in Azamgarh and 20,000 around the country. The stories these grateful farmers tell are incredibly moving and a testament to the sustainability of organic farming—constant enrichment of the soil, healthier livestock, fewer miscarriages, and thriving children. Says Kailash Nath Singh, "Organic farming has come as a real blessing for our family. Our succeeding generations will reap the benefits and realize how the land has not lost its fertility due to heavy use of chemicals."

I can't tell you how inspiring it was for Margaret and me to see women and men working in organic tulsi, psyllium, and intoxicatingly fragrant rose fields (used in their fabulous Tulsi Sweet Rose Tea), cultivating their crops in a sustainable way. They are literally healing the Earth one field at a time. Says Bharat Mitra, "It's not only that they have sustainable income, not only that the environment is healthy, not only that their livestock is doing well, not only their own health has improved so significantly, but they have the dignity of being farmers again. How beautiful. How natural. How simple."

The farmers' crops are processed and shipped from Lucknow all over the world to consumers (like Margaret and me) clamoring for organic products, which means that ORGANIC INDIA is now making a global impact as well. The company is committed to its vision of being a vehicle of consciousness; it is running its business in a way that benefits everyone who works at the company *and* the consumers who buy its high-quality products. Says Bhavani, "Unless we all experience that we are all of the same consciousness we're going to treat each other as if you don't matter."

Bharat Mitra and Bhavani's newest project is AHIMSA (Association for Holistic Integrative Medical Science in Action), an independent research foundation formed by a collaboration of "integrative medical professionals, scientists, researchers, and visionary social entrepreneurs" all operating from their hearts and minds with noble gas–like integrity (balance) and passion (energy). As with a laser, the goal of the AHIMSA community's "excimers" is to stimulate enlightenment in the world. With selfless love, they want to "liberate" health care from corporate financial interests by providing independent, evidence-based research on holistic remedies that "support, inspire, and promote True Wellness among all people."

Margaret and I were honored with an invitation to join AHIMSA, and we're especially impressed with its long view of evolutionary progress. One of the questions built into the planning process is sustainability:

"How will AHIMSA look to the grandchildren of our grandchildren?" This is a perspective that was missing from the unsustainable "Green" farming revolution, and we're happy to be part of a group that takes the long view about the health of individuals and this planet.

Conscious Parenting

I'm the first to admit that I wasn't ready to be a parent and that I was ignorant about the importance of parents (versus genes) in child development. With 20/20 hindsight, there are many things as a father I'd like to go back and change. Now when I see my daughters and sons-in-law raising their children consciously, in a way that means that these children, unlike their grandfather, won't have to rewrite a lot of negative programming, I wonder how I could have been so ignorant. I'm reminded of Bharat Mitra's description of organic farming, which could also serve as a description of conscious parenting: "How beautiful. How natural. How simple."

So simple that British psychotherapist Sue Gerhardt in *Why Love Matters: How Affection Shapes a Baby's Brain* couldn't be more correct when she writes, "Most of all, my research leads me to believe that, if the will and resources were available, the harm done to one generation need not be transmitted to the next: a damaged child need not inevitably become a damaging parent."[4]

There is nothing inevitable about generation after generation of bad parenting, and the importance of breaking this cycle cannot be overestimated. In the previous chapter, I talked about how negative programming can undermine relationships, but I didn't talk about how profound an impact good parenting can make on our violence-torn planet!

In the 1990s James W. Prescott, former director of the National Institutes of Health's section on Child Health and Human Development, concluded that the most peaceful cultures on Earth feature parents who maintain extensive physical, loving contact with their children (for example, carrying their babies on their chests and backs throughout the day). In addition, these cultures do not suppress adolescent sexuality, viewing it instead as a natural state of development that prepares adolescents for successful adult relationships. He also found that children (and animals) that do not experience loving touch are unable to suppress their stress hormones, an inability that is a harbinger of violent behavior. Says Prescott, "As a developmental neuropsychologist, I have devoted a great deal of study to the peculiar relationship between violence and pleasure. I am now convinced that the deprivation of physical sensory pleasure is the principal root cause of violence."[5]

Prescott's persuasive research has been ignored in "advanced" societies where the natural process of birth has been medicalized; where newborns are separated from their parents for extended periods; where parents are told to let infants cry for fear of spoiling them; where parents goad young children to achieve more by telling them they're not good enough; where parents, believing that genes are destiny, let children develop on their own. All of these unnatural parenting behaviors are a recipe for continued violence on this planet.

It has been an uphill struggle to focus public awareness on the fact that individual empowerment, conscious parenting, and planetary peace are connected, even though those connections are proven by solid research. But I do believe that in the face of current global crises, the message of peace and holism, which is grounded in modern revisions of traditional scientific thought, is finally being heard. One indication of increasing public awareness is that a version of the "new science," an integration of quantum physics, epigenetics, and conscious parenting I described in *The Biology of Belief,* received two awards in recognition of its ability to create peace in this world.

The first was the 2009 Goi Peace Award presented annually for "outstanding contributions toward the realization of a peaceful and harmonious world for all life on earth." Hiroo Saionji, president of the Goi Peace Foundation, made it clear that the "new science's" message of individual empowerment is more than *individual* empowerment: "[This] research . . . has contributed to a greater understanding of life and the true nature of humanity, empowering wide layers of the public to take control of their own lives and become responsible co-creators of a harmonious planetary future." The second public recognition of the "new science" was the 2012 Thousand Peace Flags award from the United Nations–sponsored Argentinean Mil Milenios de Paz (A Thousand Millennia of Peace) and Fundación PEA (Peace, Ecology & Art Foundation) organizations.

It is easy to get mired in our own personal dramas and our own efforts to build successful relationships, but these awards put such dramas into a much larger and more meaningful context. The promise of the "new science" is not only a world where there are no codependent relationships and no need to grapple with four minds in a relationship but also a world without violence, because all children receive the nurturing they need to thrive and create a better world.

Connecting Noble Gases

While preparing to write this book, I asked my online community if anyone had applied the principles offered in *The Biology of Belief* to their relationships. The large number of positive responses, and in particular this eloquent letter, blew me away:

> Hi Bruce,
>
> Here's how *The Biology of Belief* changed my relationship with my husband forever:
>
> I sat on the soft vinyl seat gazing out the window as the light played on the water outside. The train picked up speed as we glided along the tracks from Portland to Bellingham. All I could hear was Bruce's voice as I listened to his audio version of *The Biology of Belief.* I made a mental list of all the high points to tell my husband, Martin, when I returned. He was waiting for me at the train station, and before I could speak he told me about the great book he had just finished called *The Biology of Belief.*
>
> This was a watershed moment for us. We decided that it was time to change

the "track" of the tapes that played in our heads. I took a PSYCH-K workshop as one of the ways that Bruce suggested we reprogram our subconscious minds (aka our tapes), and I taught Martin.

We made a list of tapes that often played in our heads and used the PSYCH-K muscle-testing process to balance them. When we started the process, we lived mainly in the world of work with very little time for each other. We thought this was just normal and didn't realize the distance that was growing between us. Through our old belief "tapes" we were setting ourselves on a relationship course that was modeled by our parents. I could picture us in later years wondering what happened as we became strangers to each other.

Now, we were letting go of tapes that didn't serve us and recording new ones that did! Through our awareness of this reprogramming, we started charting a new path. We moved to a place with a slower pace and decided to create jobs that embraced our creativity. A year ago I would have never thought we could have come up with this: http://kck.st/ybaRPo.

Our relationship is much richer now, and I feel that we are on the same

> wavelength when we see old tapes surfacing. We are empowered to address those tapes and work together to continue charting our best life.
>
> Marcy Criner

When we followed up with Marcy before publication of this book, I learned that the project she and her husband listed on the website Kickstarter, an iPad app to enable kids to write and illustrate stories, did not get funded.

Undaunted, Marcy and Martin didn't engage in recrimination: "*You* should have done this . . . No, *you* should have done that." Instead, they decided to come up with a new project (an online course) that doesn't need outside funding. Marcy says that because she and her husband were no longer modeling their parents' relationships and had instead created a relationship their conscious minds had chosen, they were able to deal with the fact that their project didn't get funded: "We were able to not blame each other. We actually smiled and drew pictures of the lessons we learned through the project."

In fact, Marcy and Martin have come to believe that the project *was* a success because through Kickstarter they connected with a number of people who provided encouragement: "It turned out not to be about money. It was about people coming together to support us in our vision." This is another example of noble-gas communities sharing light.

The Internet is akin to the human body's nervous system because it has the potential to connect seven billion individual human beings together into one living organism called humanity. I can't say that I know how the Internet is going to evolve (any more than I know exactly the specifics of how the planet is going to evolve), but I do know that noble gases who start an organization like AHIMSA or a revolt like the Arab Spring can, through the Internet, turn their movements into global ones at breathtaking speed. Increasingly, those who recognize the importance of creating a harmonious global community are using the Internet to connect humanity. That includes me. I've decided to take my own advice and not sit in an easy chair waiting for the next stage of evolution but instead exploit the power of the Internet sitting at my computer chair. I want to help connect noble gases all over the planet, not just through my books and lectures but through my website. If you have a story to tell and would love to share it with a world seeking hope and light, please send it to me at bruce@brucelipton.com so we can post it. Through the Internet, we can build energy among one another that will make Gaia glow.

Sounds great, Bruce, some of you are thinking, *but are you sure Gaia is going to survive?* It's a question I get a lot, especially from people who are discouraged about the chaos of today's world. I am not a Pollyanna, but as I said earlier, I am optimistic because I have had the privilege of meeting so many noble gases through my work: people who are individually and collectively lighting up the world. And as I explained in the first chapter, there are repetitive fractal patterns in Nature and in evolution that offer insight, hope, and vision for a sustainable future.

The crises we're experiencing will, I believe, force evolutionary change as crises have in the past, though I also believe that it's going to be a bumpy ride up the next rung of the evolutionary ladder. At the moment, we're witnessing the disassembly of the structures people once considered solid, including religious, political, economic, and academic ones. Because they are locked into old and flawed belief systems, I believe they *need* to collapse so we can move past their limiting beliefs, like the "I beat you before you beat me" survival-of-the-fittest ethic, or the belief that humans are the result of random mutations, or the notion that genes control our lives—outdated beliefs that we have been laboring under for 150 years.

I sit here looking at the crises facing humanity and I'm excited because I believe they're a sign that we're on our way to the next level of evolution, a new belief system that will shape a civilization based on harmony and self-empowerment. I can't describe the exact consequences if and when seven billion humans decide to stop killing one another and the planet and take responsibility for the superorganism called humanity any more than an amoeba could have predicted what would happen when 50 trillion of them cooperated to form a human being! If you had asked an amoeba what would happen, there's no way it could have imagined a rocket ship to the moon or cell phones or televisions. Similarly, it's impossible to predict what will happen once seven billion humans collectively recognize that they are part of humanity, a larger enlightened superorganism. But I do know that it will be wonderful because human consciousness is one of the most powerful elements influencing the evolution of this planet.

During this time of chaos, I advise you to avoid the temptation of isolating yourself, allowing your biological drive for protection to trump your biological drive for growth. This is a time for growth, a time for taking things in, not walling yourself off. By all means take steps to protect yourself (I am storing extra food), but don't stop at protection. Reaching out to connect with others will help bring about change.

I use the analogy of the metamorphosis of a caterpillar to describe where we are now. Under the skin of a caterpillar are 6 to 7 billion cells. Every cell is a sentient entity and, in fact, the equivalent of a functional miniature human being. Every cell has a job. Some are working in the digestive system, some in the muscular system, and so on. Every cell is "employed" and getting "paid." The caterpillar is growing. Its economy is growing. Everything's in a state of luxuriant growth—happy days are here.

Then one day the caterpillar stops taking in food and stops moving. Inside the world of the caterpillar, the cells start looking around and saying, "What's going on?" The digestive cells get laid off because there hasn't been any food coming in for a while. Muscle cells lose their job when the caterpillar stops moving. Then all the cells start getting laid off. The structure they lived in and created as a community is falling apart. The cells start to panic; many commit suicide (apoptosis). The highly organized structure that was the caterpillar becomes a soup of cells disconnected from the structure. "Oh my God—this whole thing is falling apart!"

But some cells, genetically identical to the panicked cells, respond in a different way. Right in the midst of the chaos, these imaginal cells see a different vision and they become the leaders that create that new vision. All of a sudden cells come together again, this time to create something more advanced than a caterpillar; a gorgeous, soaring butterfly emerges from the soup.

I think humanity is now in "late caterpillar" when visionary imaginal cells (aka noble gases) are leading the way to a better future. I can't help but believe that the number of these imaginal cells/noble gases will reach such a critical mass that our planet will heal and evolve to a higher order of life. I envision verdant, organic fields, loving parents, Happily Ever After couples, and an amazing new butterfly that emits laser light.

EPILOGUE

Happily Ever After

A Romantic Comedy
Starring Bruce and Margaret

Scene 1: Girl Meets Boy

I do believe I loved you from the moment I laid eyes on you . . . and knowing you over the last year and a half has given time, space, energy, and real substance to my love and has fed and nourished my soul. I guess that makes you Soul Food!
I love you,
Margaret

— From the Margaret-Bruce Love Letters Archive

Margaret: Just like in the movies, it was love at first sight across a crowded room. Or more accurately, it was love at first jolt across a crowded room, a jolt that literally took my breath away.

Walking back to my front-row seat at the 1995 international conference of the Association for Perinatal and Prenatal Health, I saw the founder of the organization, Thomas Verny, speaking to someone whose back was turned to me. As I passed by the stranger, I let out an involuntary gasp and reflexively put my hand over my heart, where I had felt a jolt of energy.

I stopped walking and looked back. Thomas and the stranger were looking curiously at me, the source of the loud gasp that had taken them by surprise as much as it had taken me! I managed to blurt out, "Hi."

I made my way to my chair, asking myself, *Wow, whoa, what was* that *about?* The meeting room at the San Francisco Cathedral Hill Hotel filled up around me with hundreds of attendees, but I didn't even notice. I was staring at the floor, trying to recover from my heart jolt. This was beyond attraction, beyond lust—this was good vibrations taken to a whole new level. I hadn't even seen his face!

Finally, I looked up and discovered that the stranger was one of the speakers on the next panel and his name was Bruce Lipton. At the end of the session, after Bruce had galvanized the crowd, I literally had to push my way to the front of the line of people crowding around him, all the while revving myself up: *Margaret, this is no time to be coy. You have to go meet this guy.* I reached Bruce just as he was giving his home address to a woman who wanted to send him a check for one of his videotape lectures. When he got to La Honda, California, I blurted out, "You live in La Honda? I live in La Honda!"

So now I had had this incredible physical, visceral reaction when I walked behind this person *and* he lived only minutes away from me in the tiny town of La Honda.

Not long before that conference I had decided to open myself up to exploring (for the first time) a fully committed, communicative, and expressive relationship, but, because I'd never had one, I had no clue how to go about it. So I appealed (not for the first time) to the Universe: "All right, Universe, I want a sign, a sign so clear that I'll do something about it!" I was convinced I had gotten my sign!

Like Bruce, I was reinventing myself; we had both stepped off the edge of our known worlds. I had left an intense and rewarding 16-year career at the Summit Organization, a leader in the California human potential movement. I had also left a 13-year relationship with my mentor, who founded Summit. Leaving the Summit family where I had grown up (I started in my 20s and left when I was 39) was wrenching. And when the company I helped build folded shortly after I left and my husband died (we were separated), I could no longer avoid the reality that the old life I had loved was over.

At Summit, we offered experiential workshops, and our core message will be familiar to those who follow Bruce's work: "You are responsible for your life." In fact, the first time I heard Bruce speak, he was explaining the work I had done for 16 years in a way I had never heard before. I used the "processing" language of the human potential movement, and Bruce used the language of cell biology and quantum physics, but I realized with excitement (yet another reason to believe I had gotten my sign from the Universe) that we were talking about the same thing!

I loved my work at Summit, I loved our clients, and I loved my colleagues, all of whom were, like me, zealous practitioners of self-inquiry—we were just as committed as our clients were to figuring out why our lives didn't match the lives we said we wanted. Unsurprisingly, given my passion for internal work, my goal after I left Summit was to "process" (there's that word again) what I had gone through so I'd glean all the wisdom I could from it and walk into the next chapter of my life with an open heart.

But the first order of business was decompression. It was a joy just to sit and linger over a cup of coffee without having to run to the next appointment on my calendar, the next phone call, the next workshop booked a year in advance. I told friends I was going to revel in my free time and independence. When they told me they hoped I would find a new partner, I blithely joked that they shouldn't wish me a good relationship, just some good sex and a lot of fun.

That all changed when I arranged a mentorship with Kathlyn and Gay Hendricks, who use body-centered techniques to unravel what's truly going on with individuals and couples. The Hendrickses had been together for 20 years, but they could have been honeymooners—it was so apparent how much they liked, loved, appreciated, and honored each other. They are committed to what they call "emotional transparency" and define this as "the ability to know your own feelings and to talk about them so that others understand them."

In my work with Kathlyn and Gay, I realized that despite my stated desire for intimacy, in relationships I had always had one eye on a side-door escape. I knew I didn't need that kind of relationship again—I could do just fine on my own. But the Hendrickses inspired me to dream about moving beyond my pattern of being with men I had to drag kicking and screaming into intimacy. I opened myself up to the possibility of what I called Big Love.

Scene 2: Boy Loses Girl

Dearest Wonderful,
Thank you for loving me so well . . . even if I didn't behave in a manner suitable for such love.
I love you a ***lot!***
Brucie

—From the Bruce-Margaret Love Letter Archives

Bruce: You're probably thinking that after Margaret's love-at-first jolt, she and I, two noble gases who had dealt with their negative programming (and in one case even lectured regularly on its power to prevent you from creating the life you want), quickly experienced bliss.

Well, not exactly. We call our relationship a romantic comedy for a reason—the first "hour and a half" (actually six months) included a series of mishaps and lines in the sand more characteristic of high-level diplomacy than Happily Ever After, as well as lots and lots of joy and laughter.

Margaret's heart jolt made total sense to me, which of course won't surprise you because you've read Chapter 2. All organisms, you'll remember, broadcast unique vibratory signatures. In this case, Margaret created a specific and unique vision in her mind when she was working with the Hendrickses, a neurological vision with unique brain frequencies. She then tasked the Universe, aka her supercomputer subconscious, with a search request to alert her when the correct harmonic vibration entered her field. When she walked behind me, Margaret "read" an energy signature emanating from me that locked in (harmonically . . . this is a good vibrations story) with the frequency her subconscious was seeking.

The fact that Margaret reflexively clutched her heart at that instant also made sense to me, because I believe the heart is the receiving and responding organ that reads our energy fields. When I had my cell-mem-Brain epiphany in the Caribbean that I describe in *The Biology of Belief,* it was my heart that responded instantly in that amazing moment of awareness. In fact, I often refer to that moment as my "heart orgasm"—it was not only a moment when I "got it" but also a moment that woke me up to my heart's ability to sense Truth.

While I understood Margaret's heart jolt, I did not have the same experience when I met her. I knew I was drawn to an attractive, interesting, powerful, refreshingly direct and honest woman, but I did not yet know what is now so obvious to me—I had met the love of my life!

As I explained in the Introduction, when it comes to relationships, I am not a quick learner; actually, I'm a stay-after-school, write-on-the-blackboard-a-thousand-times kind of learner. I had made incredible progress

undoing my programming, progress that I know enabled Margaret to come into my life. But vestiges of my programming still held me back. I wanted an honest relationship, *and* I still wanted a relationship that didn't require me to edit even one word of my 17-year mantra: "I will never get married again!"

In retrospect, I realize I made what could have wound up being the dumbest move of my life—I let her go! I didn't want to mislead Margaret, so I told her I wasn't committed-relationship material.

Scenes 3 and 4: Boy and Girl Begin Their Journey

Being with you has opened up my love and I want to
continue to expand in this wonderful love I have
with you and for you . . . I love waking up
with you and talking, giggling, and loving.
I love your silliness. I love your laugh.
I love our BIG FUN with each other.
I love you, my darling,
Margaret

—From the Margaret-Bruce
Love Letters Archive

Margaret: When I heard from Bruce, or thought I heard from Bruce, that he wasn't available, I did the right thing under the circumstances—I wished him a good life. But then I cried for days as if I had lost the love of my life, quite odd behavior (though not when you consider Bruce's quantum physics explanation earlier) given that I had only talked to Bruce for a total of a few minutes!

Of course, it didn't end there. After a few more twists and turns (all grist for Scene 3 of our romantic comedy), we started dating. But we still weren't exactly on an inexorable Happily Ever After trajectory.

Every time we had a date, Bruce would repeat his disclaimer that he wasn't relationship material and just in case I hadn't gotten the message, he made sure we met at *his* house and *he* cooked the meals; he didn't want to be "beholden" to me lest that smack of a permanent commitment.

After lots of soul searching, I overcame my qualms about exploring a commitment-free relationship with Bruce and decided I would take the risk of getting my heart broken. I vowed to learn everything I could about being fully present with another person (I gave up on the "fully committed" part of Big Love but not the emotional transparency part) for as long as our relationship lasted. So after I sat through Bruce's disclaimer every week, we would move on to my emotional transparency agenda, which was all about communicating honestly: "There's something we need to talk about . . ."

What I soon learned, to my surprise, was that though I was definitely the more intense, serious one on the surface, I had met my match. Bruce's big brain and big heart meant that I had to become more expansive to keep up with him. I started learning so much about how to express love. And more surprising, I learned a lot about commitment without his ever using that word. In truth, despite my passion for self-inquiry, emotional transparency was exhausting for me at first. It required being present all the time, even the times I wanted to space out and not pay attention for a while. The temptation was to say at some point, "This is too much trouble."

Instead, I chose to continue and focused on enjoying our glorious time together—Bruce is so endearingly funny and sweet. We had (and still have) a lot of silliness, a lot of giggles, and a lot of laughter. One of Bruce's neighbors said she loved to visit her horses who grazed in front of his house (La Honda is rural) because she'd hear our laughter and it made her happy, too.

The laughter started early, even before I had made peace with Bruce's commitment disclaimer. On one of our first dates, Bruce suggested a game of Scrabble. What Bruce was soon to learn was that I *love* Scrabble and I play it mercilessly to win! When I beat him, he was in total shock and very impressed that I had bested his formidable vocabulary. I told him I would have suggested a game the first time we met had I known how much my Scrabble playing would impress him.

Actually, the way I beat Bruce was not by besting his vocabulary but by using obscure two- and three-letter Scrabble words I had long since memorized—one of my favorites is *oe,* a violent Faroe Islands whirlwind. Bruce launched into a comic presentation of my win filled with the ridiculous words I had beaten him with that was so funny I was rolling on the floor laughing. Beating me became a challenge for him and when he finally did, I said, "How refreshing!"

We were having fun, and we were also communicating on a deep level. For Bruce, life had been serious for too many years when he was following someone else's script for a happy life. And I realized that I needed to lighten up and soften my language after a 16-year career dedicated to confronting things *now.*

Our friends started noticing how good we were (and are) together. Bruce's friends, who knew about his commitment phobia, were telling him not to do anything to ruin our relationship—one told him not to come back unless he brought me with him. My longtime friends were telling me that they had never seen a partner who matched my high energy levels so well.

Despite Bruce's need to repeat his disclaimer and my need to push my emotional transparency agenda too hard and too fast (lest I get stuck with another man who didn't want to deal with his "shit," to put it indelicately), on some level, like our friends, I believe we knew we had started our journey to Happily Ever After.

Scene 5, etc.: The Bumpy Course to Happily Ever After

The course of true love never did run smooth.

— *A Midsummer Night's Dream* by William Shakespeare

Margaret: Of course, it still wasn't a straight path to Happily Ever After.

People always ask me if Bruce and I argue, and I tell them at the beginning we certainly did—and in ways that would be familiar to lots of couples. And then I tell the story of our pre-GPS road trip.

It wasn't a long trip; we were only driving for about two hours to visit friends. But we got lost. I kept suggesting that we stop for directions and Bruce kept making turns and trying to figure it out. Yes [sigh], I know, stereotypical male-female responses! I said something like "That's not what I would do" but by then Bruce was so

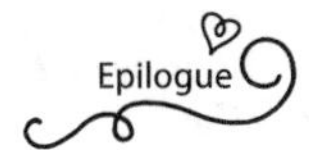

irritated with me and with himself that he pulled into a shopping mall parking lot, got out, and said, "Fine, you drive." Then (in public) we were nose to nose and yelling at each other, telling each other what to do and where to go.

After a few seconds of that fierce confrontation, we stopped, stepped away from each other, took deep breaths, let out sounds like "Phew!" and "Whoa!" and got back in the car. We were silent for a long while. Then we started to talk about the amazingly strong knee-jerk reactions we had both had, how bad they felt, and how they were not what either of us wanted. This was the exact opposite of the good-vibrations heart jolt I had experienced at the Cathedral Hill Hotel. This was a textbook case of bad vibrations! In fact, it took almost a week (Bruce remembers two weeks) before the "bad" vibes dissipated. During that time we agreed that *that* would never happen again. We had both been in *those* kinds of volatile, destructive relationships in the past, and it was *really* clear to us that we were *not* going to do that ever again.

At the time, it was a shock that we could still degenerate so quickly into intense anger. But now, with the perspective of years of living Happily Ever After, I think it isn't possible to have a really intimate relationship without some dark stuff coming up—the kind of anger that makes you want your partner to suffer a little to make a point, the kind of hurt feelings that make you want to exact revenge.

After our parking-lot confrontation, we asked ourselves whether we wanted to be right all the time or whether we wanted to have a relationship. We chose our relationship. Then we consciously and subconsciously (we're always cognizant of our four minds) decided to take responsibility for being control freaks and work on ways to let go of our need to be right all the time!

First, I came up with a technique for curbing my tendency to speak critically at emotionally charged moments. I think it's a pattern we're all familiar with. You know that what you *want* to say will add salt to the wound so you vow not to say it. But you blurt it out anyway (that corrosive subconscious programming) because you *know* you're right and your partner is wrong. The way I subdued the critical chatter bursting to come forth was to go into the bathroom, look at myself in the mirror, and have an eye-to-eye talk with myself: "Margaret, do you want to be right, or do you want to be in love?" It took practice, but I did it over and over and it worked. After a session at the mirror, I would walk back into the room having shifted my energy to my heart. My words were kind because I had chosen to shift my energy to unconditional love.

Bruce and I also cultivated another technique that helps us shift from hurt, anger, or fear into unconditional love. We developed a habit, which has now become automatic, of reconnecting silently with touch rather than arguing about who's right. Reconnecting means that no matter how bad you feel, no matter how much you think your partner hurt you, no matter how much you want your partner to suffer a little to make a point, you sit together without talking or arguing to reconnect on a deeper level than words. If you let go of the details of a dispute and make contact with each other, your hearts open again and everything gets handled really quickly. You do have to make sure you're touching—knees,

hands, arms. Without touching you could wind up just sitting there stewing!

We also got into the now automatic habit of using loving words to reconnect throughout each day, even when Bruce is on the road lecturing and we have to do it via Skype. We say "I love you" all the time—when we pass in the hallway, when one of us leaves the house, etc. We liberally use endearing silly nicknames (invented by Bruce) like "Goosie, Brucie." And we also make sure we have lots of physical reassurance every day: lots of hugs, and smooches that provided another silly nickname, "The Schmoochilinis."

If you're thinking this sounds a tad over the top, you're not the first. Sally Thomas, who works with me at Mountain of Love Productions, says that when she first met us she thought the constant "I love you"s were too "syrupy." Then she started to appreciate them: "No matter how stressful things get, Bruce and Margaret always use accepting and loving and kind communication. They don't hold on to things and become resentful. The Honeymoon Effect has not worn off." Then she started to imitate us. "The funny thing is that it rubbed off on me. It's a good way to be when you're with somebody and they're driving you crazy—you just have to remember you love them to death."

For my part, I think constant reinforcement is a good thing. I do not take our Happily Ever After for granted! Like Bruce's, my nuclear family did not model positive relationships. I left home at 16 knowing I could take care of myself better than I was cared for at home because I was the adult in the house. I believe that our romantic comedy could have turned into a tragedy had *both* of us not been aware of our negative programming, taken steps to overcome it, and reinforced our love with supportive and appreciative words (and deeds) every day.

In the end, good vibrations aren't enough, which won't surprise anyone who has read this book! I've met people who were convinced they were soul mates because they were so attuned energetically, but their relationships didn't work out, at least in this lifetime. Before we could move on to Happily Ever After, we both needed to deal with the invisible baggage that was holding us back.

Final Scene: Happily Ever After

Your beauty illuminates my life—I am so dearly in love with you! I truly understand the idea of Heaven—for you have completed my understanding.
With love for you, my dearest Gooselini,
Brucie

—From the Bruce-Margaret Love Letter Archives

Bruce: So I told you I'm a slow learner, but in this case not that slow!

Six months after we met, we were sitting in the living room, Margaret on the sofa and me on the floor leaning against the sofa, when I started to laugh, then caught myself and stopped. Margaret kept asking what I had started to laugh about. Eventually, I told her I had almost blurted out, "Margaret, will you marry me?" Margaret's response to this momentous news that followed 17 years of repeating my "I will never marry again" mantra was

"Yeah, riiiight." In fact, that was her response for the entire week it took me to convince her I was serious!

Finally, I had realized that Margaret was the woman I wanted to be with. Finally, I had realized that I was already living the relationship I had longed for. We were sharing everything and that included and still includes the bacon—if there are four pieces, she gets two! We were having fun and we were as intimate as could be.

Though it was a milestone, letting go of my "never get married again" shaving mantra turned out to be a natural progression I didn't have to think about much. The turning point for me came when I realized that I trusted Margaret with my life. I knew in my heart that if I needed somebody to make a decision about my life when I was incapacitated, she was the only one I would trust to make it. In my entire existence on this planet, I had never had that sense that I could turn over my life to someone else if necessary. To me, that realization was mind-boggling—I had come to trust her that much.

When I convinced Margaret I was serious about my new level of trust (and serious about not needing to repeat my disclaimer anymore), we decided to commit to an experiment in Happily Ever After. The experiment/challenge was to continue what we were doing without any end goal. Instead, we committed to a Zenlike Happily Ever After experiment, a "be here now" experiment without any long-term goals. Seventeen years later (and counting), our Happily-Ever-After living-in-the-moment experiment is still going strong.

Like Margaret, I don't think our experiment was necessarily ordained to succeed. We had a great start, but if we hadn't made course corrections, if we hadn't dealt with lingering unconscious behaviors, I don't think we would have made it.

Margaret has already described some of the habits of loving communication that we took time to embed in our subconscious. I think the "Honeymoon Weekends" we set aside for ourselves were crucial as well. They were three days (soon extended to four days when our schedules allowed) of cocooning, leaving behind the "real" world in favor of our woodsy mountain retreat. Even now that we're busier and can't always arrange for those weekends, we still have that access point, that love and joy with and for each other that we experienced during those weekends early in our relationship and still experience today.

Sometimes I confess I can't help but wish we could have experienced that love and joy when we were young. I once told Margaret that had we met in high school we would have been high school sweethearts. She was touched, but then we thought about it and came to the conclusion that it wouldn't have worked. Had we met in high school, that pre-GPS road trip might not have been a one-time occurrence—we both had a lot to learn (actually a lot of subconscious programming to undo) before we stopped our wobbly, codependent spinning and became noble gases!

As I learned again and again in my life, until you get your own act together, you're not ready for Big Love. What you're ready for is one of those codependent relationships where you *desperately need* a partner. (Remember the woman in the Caribbean who correctly told me I was too needy.) When you learn to spin in balance on your own like a noble gas, Big Love becomes possible. In my case, I experienced 40 years of anxiety, though

I have to tell you that now that I'm here, they are irrelevant. It was worth everything to get here!

I hope that by reading this book you'll be able to shave a lot off your learning years—there's no reason you have to be as slow a learner as I was. Now that you know about subconscious programming and how it can undermine your life and your relationships, I hope you'll be proactive about undoing that programming, proactive about taking responsibility for the relationships you create in your life, and proactive about leaving your codependent relationships behind. By all means, if you like romantic comedies, keep watching them. But there's a huge difference between sitting and watching someone else's script and writing your own. Create your own romantic comedy starring the person you want to be and the person you attract into your life.

Writing your own Happily Ever After script means no more victimology, no more narratives of the sort I used to create like "She did me wrong." And please, no guilt for past relationships! How were you to know that invisible programming, which you had nothing to do with, was undermining your relationships?

Move on and seize every moment of today. Let go of yesterday! And no excuses! If Margaret and I, who come from Dysfunctional Street, USA, can make it work, so can you. Of course, if you're one of those lucky couples who met in second grade, fell in love in high school, and are thriving in adulthood, mazel tov! You don't need excuses or inspiration, at least in the relationship area of your life; your four minds are already aligned.

Though I hope we can provide inspiration, Margaret and I cannot provide a blueprint for a Happily Ever After relationship because there is no one-size-fits-all formula for creating Happily Ever After. Margaret and I, as you now know, took completely different pathways to get to the point where we were ready to create our Happily Ever After. Though I can't offer you a blueprint, I can offer you some resources and a handy Honeymoon Effect checklist in the Appendix that follows this Epilogue.

I also can't offer you perfection. Happily Ever After doesn't mean that I'm perfect or that everything is perfect in my life. What it does mean is that I've reinvented myself and my life. I'm living in the same world, but it's really not the same world I used to live in. Things (like leaky roofs, parking tickets, and the deadline for this book) that used to discombobulate me don't turn me upside down, and they don't throw our relationship off balance either. Margaret and I never lose our love no matter what other things are going on in our lives. Whatever happens, it's okay.

What I can offer you is hope for a better world.

When you create a Happily Ever After relationship, you start attracting like-minded people who form a buffer between you and the other part of the world you used to be in the trenches with. You create your own bubble filled with the glow of noble gases: those "enlightened" noble gases from Chapter 5; that is, people who know there is another way to live.

I believe that if our lives hadn't become distorted by programming, the entire planet would be part of this bubble. The entire planet would glow like a laser because it would be a planet filled with love. Albert Einstein once said, "There are two ways to live your life. One is as though nothing is a miracle. The other is as though everything is a miracle." Create your own light and share

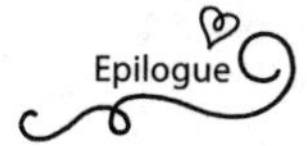

it with your partner and with others so this planet will glow with the laser light of noble gases, who every day create Heaven on Earth. Like my hero Einstein, noble gases know that we can live our lives like the miracles they are.

APPENDIX A

The Honeymoon Effect Checklist

1. Conscious mind review: Be "conscious" of what you ask for . . .
2. Subconscious mind review: Be aware of the programming you received before you could consciously "think" about it.
3. Take advantage of tools to reprogram your subconscious, including energy psychology (aka super learning), hypnosis, subliminal tapes, and mindfulness (living in the moment).
4. Practice daily random acts of kindness and frequent terms of endearment, and tailor them to your relationship.

5. Open your heart to your partner when you have a dispute or want to bring the Honeymoon Effect back into your relationship by opting out of verbal arguments using silence and physical touching.
6. Change your own life first so you can attract a partner who is an excitable noble gas.

APPENDIX B

Comedies for Cinematherapy

(in alphabetical order)

Amélie

As Good As It Gets

Blast from the Past

Bridget Jones's Diary

Continental Divide

Defending Your Life

Definitely, Maybe

Doc Hollywood

Educating Rita

Groundhog Day

High Fidelity
It Could Happen to You
Jerry Maguire
Love Actually
Moonstruck
My Big Fat Greek Wedding
New in Town
Sleepless in Seattle
Splash
The 40-Year-Old Virgin
The American President
The Goodbye Girl
Today's Special
When Harry Met Sally

RESOURCES

Belief Change Modalities for Accessing and Reprogramming Your Subconscious Mind

(In alphabetical order)

Alchemical Healing (www.shamanicjourneys.com)

Alchemical Healing combines innovative methods from shamanism and energetic healing with the principles of alchemy to create physical healing, therapeutic counseling, and spiritual growth.

Alchemy Techniques (www.alchemytechniques.com)

Alchemy Techniques is a collection of techniques to integrate all aspects of the self in the deepest layer of the heart (center).

The Body Code System of Natural Healing (www.drbradleynelson.com)

The Body Code System for Ultimate Energy Healing and Body Balancing is a program to find and correct underlying imbalances that block health and happiness.

Body Talk System (www.bodytalksystem.com)

BodyTalk is designed to resynchronize the body's energy systems so they can operate as nature intended.

Consciousness 2.0 (consciousness2-0.com)

Consciousness 2.0 is a self-guided program to upgrade destructive programming by "uninstalling" fear, judgment, limitation, struggle, and pain and "installing" each person's highest self consciousness.

Core Health (www.corehealth.us)

Core Health's DTQ (Deeply, Thoroughly, Quickly) is a process to permanently reactivate a person's innate healthy core.

EMDR (www.emdr.com)

EMDR is a psychotherapy that enables people to heal more quickly than traditional therapy from the symptoms and emotional distress that result from disturbing life experiences.

Emotional Freedom Techniques (www.eftfree.net)

Based on new discoveries about the body's subtle energies, Emotional Freedom Techniques are used as therapy for emotional, health, and performance issues.

The Healing Codes (www.thehealingcode.com/home.php)

The Healing Codes are designed to remove stress from the body, thus allowing the neuroimmune system to heal whatever is wrong in the body.

The Hendricks Institute (www.hendricks.com)

The Hendricks Institute is an international learning center that teaches core skills for conscious living and conscious loving and is committed to creating a worldwide community of people who want to explore new heights of love, creativity, and well-being.

Holographic Repatterning (www.repatterning.org)

Resonance Repatterning is a system to identify and clear the patterns of energy underlying any issue, problem, or pain you are experiencing.

Holosync (www.centerpointe.com)

Holosync is a form of neuroaudio technology for creating a balance between brain hemispheres to enhance mental/emotional health and mental functioning.

Inner Resonance Technologies (www.innerresonance.com)

Inner Resonance features seven steps designed to allow each person's automatic system to rebalance and harmonize physically, emotionally, mentally, and spiritually.

Instant Emotional Healing (www.instantemotionalhealing.com)

Instant Emotional Healing: Acupressure for the Emotions by Peter T. Lambrou, Ph.D., and George J. Pratt, Ph.D.: a book that explains the foundations of energy psychology.

The Journey (www.thejourney.com)

The Journey is designed to access the body's own healing wisdom at the deepest level of "source" or the soul.

LifeFlow Meditation (www.project-meditation.org)

Based on biofeedback research, LifeFlow Meditation places the listener into brain-wave states that enhance happiness, well-being, and learning abilities.

NetMindBody (www.netmindbody.com)

NetMindBody is a mind-body stress-reduction technique for finding and removing neurological imbalances related to unresolved mind-body issues.

Neurolink's Neurological Integration System (www.neurolinkglobal.com)

Neurolink's protocols leverage the brain's ability to restore the body and all its systems to full potential.

PSYCH-K (www.psych-k.com)

PSYCH-K is a set of principles and processes to change subconscious beliefs that limit the expression of your full potential as a divine being that is having a human experience.

Rapid Eye Technology (www.rapideyetechnology.com)

Rapid Eye Technology releases stress and trauma (without reliving the trauma) by simulating REM sleep, your body's own natural release system.

Reconnective Healing (www.thereconnection.com/about)

Reconnective Healing uses vibrational frequencies to heal body, mind, and spirit.

The RIM Method (www.riminstitute.com)

The RIM Method reconstructs affirming images in cellular memory to create subconscious changes for accelerated emotional and physical well-being and greater success.

Rosen Method (www.rosenmethod.org)

The Rosen Method features gentle, direct touch to alleviate chronic muscle tension using hands that "listen rather than manipulate."

The Sedona Method (www.sedona.com)

The Sedona Method teaches people how to tap into their natural ability to release painful or unwanted feelings, beliefs, and thoughts.

Silva UltraMind ESP System (www.silvaultramindsystems.com)

The Silva UltraMind ESP is a system to unlock the incredible powers of people's minds to connect to a higher power that provides guidance for leading a happier and more successful life.

Three in One Concepts (www.3in1concepts.us)

Based on research and development in the field of applied kinesiology, Three in One Concepts assists people who want to take responsibility for creating their own well-being by integrating body, mind, and spirit.

The WOW Process (www.thewowprocess.com)

WOW is a process to alleviate physical, emotional, mental, or spiritual stress and suffering.

ENDNOTES

Chapter 1: Our Drive to Bond

1. Bruce H. Lipton, Ph.D., Steve Bhaerman, *Spontaneous Evolution* (Carlsbad, CA: Hay House, 2009), 10.

2. Lewis Thomas, *The Lives of a Cell: Notes of a Biology Watcher* (New York: Viking, 1974), 11–12.

3. Robert Sapolsky, "The Uniqueness of Humans" (Stanford University Class Day Lecture: June 13, 2009), www.youtube.com/watch?v=hrCVu25wQ5s.

4. Laura S. Scott, *Two Is Enough: A Couple's Guide to Living Childless by Choice* (Berkeley, CA: Seal Press, 2009), 1.

5. Ibid., 23–24.

6. Ibid., 77.

7. Nathan W. Bailey and Marlene Zuk, "Same-Sex Sexual Behavior and Evolution," *Trends in Ecology and Evolution,* vol. 24, no. 8 (June 10, 2009): 439–46.

8. Bruce Bagemihl, *Biological Exuberance: Animal Homosexuality and Natural Diversity* (New York: St. Martin's Press, 1999), 554.

Chapter 2: Good Vibrations

1. Vladilen S. Letokhov, "Detecting Individual Atoms and Molecules with Lasers," *Scientific American,* vol. 259, no. 3 (September 1988): 44–49.

2. Mark Hallett, "Transcranial Magnetic Stimulation and the Human Brain," *Nature,* vol. 406, no. 6792 (July 2000):147–50.

3. Allan W. Snyder and others, "Savant-like Skills Exposed in Normal People by Suppressing the Left Fronto-temporal Lobe," *Journal of Integrative Neuroscience,* vol. 2, no. 2, (December 2003): 149–58.

4. R. E. Hoffman et al., "Transcranial Magnetic Stimulation and Auditory Hallucinations in Schizophrenia," *The Lancet,* vol. 355, no. 9209 (March 25, 2000): 1073–75.

5. Women & Infants Hospital, "Efficacy of Transcranial Magnetic Stimulation for Depression Confirmed in New Study," *ScienceDaily* (July 26, 2012), www.sciencedaily.com /releases/2012/07/120726180305.htm.

6. L.=M. Duan, "Quantum Correlation Between Distant Diamonds," *Science,* vol. 334, no. 6060 (December 2, 2011): 1213–14.

7. Amit Goswami, "'Quantum Physics, Consciousness, Creativity, and Healing' with Amit Goswami [part 1 of 3]," Institute of Noetic Sciences, Audio Lectures (2006), 00:39:58, www.noetic .org/library/audio-lectures/quantum-physics-consciousness-creativity-and/.

8. J. Grinberg-Zylberbaum and others, "The Einstein-Podolsky-Rosen Paradox in the Brain: the Transferred Potential," *Physics Essays,* vol. 7, no. 4 (December 1994): 422–28.

9. Marilyn Schlitz, et al, "Of Two Minds: Skeptic-Proponent Collaboration within Parapsychology," *British Journal of Psychology,* vol. 97 (2006): 313–22.

10. Richard Conn Henry, "The Mental Universe," *Nature,* vol. 436, no. 7047 (July 7, 2005): 29.

11. David P. Barash and Judith Eve Lipton, *The Myth of Monogamy* (New York: W. H. Freeman, 2001), 10.

12. Mary Karmelek, "Was This Gazelle's Death an Accident or a Suicide?" *Scientific American* (May 24, 2011), http://blogs.scientificamerican.com/anecdotes-from-the-archive/2011/05/24/was-this-gazelles-death-an-accident-or-a-suicide.

Chapter 3: Love Potions

1. (a)Harry E. Wedeck, *A Dictionary of Aphrodisiacs* (New York: M. Evans & Company, Inc., 1992). Bruce H. Lipton, "A Fine-Structural Analysis of Normal and Modulated Cells in Myogenic Culture," *Developmental Biology*, vol. 60 (1977): 26–47. (b) ———, "Collagen Synthesis by Normal and Bromodeoxyuridine-treated Cells in Myogenic Culture," *Developmental Biology*, vol. 61 (1977): 153–65.

2. Lyle H. Miller and Alma Dell Smith, *The Stress Solution* (New York: Pocket Books, 1995), 12.

3. D. Marazziti and D. Canale, "Hormonal Changes when Falling in Love," *Psychoneuroendocrinology*, vol. 29, no. 7 (August, 2004): 931–36.

4. T. J. Loving, E. E. Crockett, and A. A. Paxson, "Passionate Love and Relationship Thinkers: Experimental Evidence for Acute Cortisol Elevations in Women," *Psychoneuroendocrinology*, vol. 34, no. 6 (July 2009): 939–46.

5. Theresa L. Crenshaw, M.D., *The Alchemy of Love and Lust: How Our Sex Hormones Influence Our Relationships* (New York: Pocket Books, 1996), 5–6.

6. Ibid., 148.

7. Ibid., 124.

8. Liza O'Donnell and others, "Estrogen and Spermatogenesis," *Endocrine Reviews*, vol. 22, no. 3 (June 1, 2001): 289–318.

9. Carl Clayton Holloway and David F. Clayton, "Estrogen Synthesis in the Male Brain Triggers Development of the Avian Song Control Pathway in Vitro," *Nature Neuroscience*, vol. 4, no. 2 (February 2001): 170–175.

10. David J. Linden, *The Compass of Pleasure: How Our Brains Make Fatty Foods, Orgasm, Exercise, Marijuana, Generosity, Vodka, Learning, and Gambling Feel So Good* (New York: Viking, 2011), 18.

11. Andrés Vidal-Gadea et al., "Caenorhabditis Elegans Selects Distinct Crawling and Swimming Gaits via Dopamine and Serotonin," *PNAS,* vol. 108, no. 42 (October 18, 2011), 17504–09.

12. Linden, *The Compass of Pleasure,* 3–5.

13. Ibid., 7–15.

14. Andreas Bartels and Semir Zeki, "The Neural Basis of Romantic Love," *NeuroReport,* vol. 11, no. 17 (November 27, 2000): 3829–34.

15. Bianca P. Acevedo and others, "Neural Correlates of Long-term, Intense Romantic Love," *Social Cognitive and Affective Neuroscience,* vol. 7, no. 2 (February 2, 2012): 145–59.

16. Lowell L. Getz and C. Sue Carter, "Prairie-vole Partnerships," *American Scientist,* vol. 84, no. 1 (January–February 1996): 56–62.

17. Larry J. Young, Anne Z. Murphy Young, and Elizabeth A. D. Hammock, "Anatomy and Neurochemistry of the Pair Bond," *The Journal of Comparative Neurology,* vol. 493, no. 1 (December 5, 2005): 51–57.

18. John M. Stribley and C. Sue Carter, "Developmental Exposure to Vasopressin Increases Aggression in Adult Prairie Voles," *PNAS,* vol. 96, no. 22 (October 26, 1999): 12601–04.

19. Thomas R. Insel, Zuo-Xin Wang, and Craig F. Ferris, "Patterns of Brain Vasopressin Receptor Distribution Associated with Social Organization in Microtine Rodents," *The Journal of Neuroscience,* vol. 14, no. 9 (September 1, 1994): 5381–92.

20. L. J. Young, D. Toloczko, and T. R. Insel, "Localization of Vasopressin (V1a) Receptor Binding and mRNA in the Rhesus Monkey Brain," *Journal of Neuroendocrinology,* vol. 11 (1999): 291–97.

21. Miranda M. Lim et al., "Enhanced Partner Preference in a Promiscuous Species by Manipulating the Expression of a Single Gene," *Nature,* vol. 429 (June 17, 2004): 754–57.

22. Yan Liu, J. Thomas Curtis, and Zuoxin Wang, "Vasopressin in the Lateral Septum Regulates Pair Bond Formation in Male Prairie Voles (*Microtus ochrogaster*)," *Behavioral Neuroscience*, vol. 115, no. 4 (2001): 910–19.

23. Thomas Insel and Terrence J. Hulihan, "A Gender-Specific Mechanism for Pair Bonding: Oxytocin and Partner Preference Formation in Monogamous Voles," *Behavioral Neuroscience*, vol. 109, no. 4 (August 1995): 782–89.

24. Beate Ditzen et al., "Intranasal Oxytocin Increases Positive Communication and Reduces Cortisol Levels During Couple Conflict," *Biological Psychiatry*, vol. 65, no. 9 (May 1, 2009): 910–19.

25. Michael Kosfeld and others, "Oxytocin Increases Trust in Humans," *Nature*, vol. 435 (June 2, 2005): 673–76.

26. Peter Kirsch and others, "Oxytocin Modulates Neural Circuitry for Social Cognition and Fear in Humans," *The Journal of Neuroscience*, vol. 25, no. 49 (December 7, 2005): 11489–93.

27. D. Marazziti and others, "Alteration of the Platelet Serotonin Transporter in Romantic Love," *Psychological Medicine*, vol. 29 (1999): 741–45.

28. Helen Fisher, *Why We Love: The Nature and Chemistry of Romantic Love* (New York: St. Martin's, 2004), 155–57.

29. Carolyn H. Declerck, Christophe Boone, and Toko Kiyonari, "Oxytocin and Cooperation under Uncertainty: The Modulating Role of Incentives and Social Information," *Hormones and Behavior*, vol. 57, no. 3 (March 2010): 368–374.

30. Carsten K. W. De Dreu et al., "Oxytocin Promotes Human Ethnocentrism," *PNAS*, vol. 108, no. 4 (January 25, 2011): 1262–66.

31. Robert M. Sapolsky, "Peace, Love and Oxytocin," *The Los Angeles Times*, December 4, 2011.

Chapter 4: Four Minds Don't Think Alike

1. Marianne Szegedy-Maszak, "Mysteries of the Mind: Your Unconscious is Making Your Everyday Decisions," *U.S. News & World Report* (February 8, 2005).

2. Tor Nørretranders, *The User Illusion: Cutting Consciousness Down to Size* (New York: Penguin, 1998), 124–25.

3. David Chamberlain, *The Mind of Your Newborn Baby* (Berkeley, CA: North Atlantic Books, 1998), xiii.

4. Thomas R. Verny, M.D., and Pamela Weintraub, *Tomorrow's Baby: The Art and Science of Parenting from Conception through Infancy* (New York: Simon & Schuster, 2002), 29.

5. Annie Murphy Paul, "Fetal Origins: How the First Nine Months Shape the Rest of Your Life," *Time* (September 22, 2010).

6. (a) R. Laibow, "Medical Applications of NeuroBioFeedback" in *Textbook of NeuroBioFeedback,* edited by J. R. Evans and A. Abarbanel (Burlington, MA: Academic Press, 1999), 83–102. (b) R. Laibow, personal communication with B. H. Lipton. New Jersey, (2002).

7. "Like Mother, Like Son," *Science,* vol. 292 (April 13, 2001), 205.

8. Suze Orman, *The 9 Steps to Financial Freedom* (New York: Crown, 1997), 12.

9. Ibid., 3.

10. Val Kinjerski, *Rethinking Your Work: Getting to the Heart of What Matters* (Chesapeake, VA: Kaizen Publishing, 2009), 117.

11. Matthew A. Killingsworth and Daniel T. Gilbert, "A Wandering Mind Is an Unhappy Mind," *Science,* vol. 330, no. 6006 (November 12, 2010): 932.

12. Bill Hendrick, "Wandering Mind May Lead to Unhappiness: Researchers Say People Are Most Happy Having Sex, Exercising, Socializing, Mainly Because Such Activities Help Keep the Mind from Wandering," *WebMD,* www.webmd.com/balance /news/20101109/wandering-mind-may-lead-to-unhappiness (November 11, 2010).

13. Jim Lagopoulos et al., "Increased Theta and Alpha EEG Activity During Nondirective Meditation," *The Journal of Alternative and Complementary Medicine,* vol. 15, no. 110 (November 2009): 1187–92.

14. Jeffrey L. Fannin and Robert M. Williams, "Leading Edge Neuroscience Reveals Significant Correlations Between Beliefs,

the Whole-Brain State, and Psychotherapy," *CQ: The CAPA Quarterly* (August 2012), 14–32.

15. Jeffrey L. Fannin and Robert M. Williams, "Neuroscience Reveals the Whole-Brain State and Its Applications for International Business and Sustainable Success," *International Journal of Management and Business,* vol. 3, no. 1 (August 2012).

Chapter 5: Noble Gases: Spreading Peace, Love, and Tulsi Tea

1. James Lovelock, *The Vanishing Face of Gaia: A Final Warning* (New York: Basic Books, 2010), 196.

2. James Lovelock, Goi Peace Prize Award 2000, "Dialogue Session: Dr. James Lovelock Meets Young People," www.goipeace.or.jp/english/activities/award/award2-1.html.

3. Alex Renton, "India's Hidden Climate Change Catastrophe," *The Independent,* August 6, 2012.

4. Sue Gerhardt, *Why Love Matters: How Affection Shapes a Baby's Brain* (New York: Brunner-Routledge, 2004), 2.

5. James W. Prescott, "Body Pleasure and the Origins of Violence," *The Bulletin of the Atomic Scientists* (November 1975): 10–20.

INDEX

C

D

E

G

H

Q

R

S

ACKNOWLEDGMENTS

My path to understanding and learning to live the Honeymoon Effect has resembled a roller-coaster ride, with extreme highs and sobering lows. On my journey, I acquired knowledge from a large number of teachers with whom I shared physical, emotional, and/or spiritual life experiences. Many were willing teachers and frankly, some were not. Yet each individual collectively contributed to the grand synthesis of this life-transforming knowledge.

First, I would like to honor some very important teachers whose wisdom has provided me with insight into the fundamental secrets of life. It is with gratitude and appreciation that I thank the stem cells in my research and the 50 trillion cells making up the community I have come to know as "Bruce." The future of human civilization is truly written in the wisdom of the cells.

Once I embarked upon the path to living Heaven on Earth, I found myself surrounded by angels, the loving celestial beings described in all religions. The word *angel* is derived from the Greek word *angelos,* which means "harbinger" or "messenger." Every angel in my life has taught me an aspect of Universal Love, which for many represents God.

An Angel of Light who has significantly contributed to and influenced the presentation of this work is Patricia A. King. Patricia is a Bay Area freelance writer and former *Newsweek* reporter who worked for a decade as the magazine's San Francisco bureau chief. She works on book projects and newspaper and magazine stories that focus on health issues, especially mind-body medicine and the role stress plays in disease. A native of Boston, Patricia lives in Marin County, California.

As I experienced in our earlier collaborative effort that resulted in the bestselling *The Biology of Belief,* I found Patricia to be a loving colleague and remarkable editor. As many will attest, I am a man of several million words, and my Angel Patricia whittled me down to the 40,000 readable, informative, and frequently humorous words in this book.

A contributing angel with an artist's flair is my dear "spiritual" son Bob Mueller, creator of the beautiful visionary art that graces the cover. As happened with *The Biology of Belief* and *Spontaneous Evolution,* I spin a tale to Bob and he weaves a visually stunning image that captures the deep essence of the work. Thank you, dear Bob—that's three winners for three covers! Bob is cofounder and creative director of Lightspeed Design in Bellevue, Washington. He and his company have produced award-winning 3-D technology and amazing light and sound shows for corporations, science museums, and planetariums around the world. Bob's creative endeavors can be sampled at www.lightspeeddesign.com.

Special appreciation goes out to the band of loving angels who gathered together to review the manuscript, critique the work, and provide invaluable feedback used in fine-tuning the text. I send love to each of the following dear and trusted friends, who played a significant and vital role in bringing this book to you. In random order, they are: Shelly Keller, Diana Sutter, Susan Payginnes, Curt Rexroth, Terry and Christine Bugno, Theresa and Vaughan Wiles, Robert and Susan Mueller, Joan Borysenko and Gordon Dveirin, Patricia Gift, Ned Leavitt, Barry and Karen Rushton, Sherry Burton, Reinhard and Michaela Fuchs, and Bhavani and Bharat Mitra Lev. Special appreciation goes out to Sally Thomas: more than a reader, she's our friend and loving colleague.

I am forever grateful for the love and support offered by my family, who stayed with me no matter how strange things had become. I acknowledge the love and appreciation for my sister, Marsha, and brother, David, for sharing the pain and laughter that marked our journey into life. I am thankful for seeing Heaven on Earth materialized in the lives of my daughter Tanya; her love, Jean-Brice; my grandchildren Jean-Gabrielle and Lily-Anabelle; and my daughter Jennifer, her life-partner Stef, and my grandson, Miles.

And the best for last . . . the message in this book and all the Heaven on Earth would be personally meaningless were it not for the love I share with my dearest friend and teacher, Margaret Horton. Margaret is my Angel of Love and Light, my inspiration and guide on this fabulous journey of awakening. The love we share is a blessing from the Universe.

ABOUT THE AUTHOR

Bruce H. Lipton, Ph.D., a pioneer in the new biology, is an internationally recognized leader in bridging science and spirit. A cell biologist by training, Bruce was on the faculty of the University of Wisconsin's School of Medicine and later performed groundbreaking stem-cell research at Stanford University. He is the best-selling author of *The Biology of Belief* and the more recent *Spontaneous Evolution,* co-authored with Steve Bhaerman. Bruce received the 2009 prestigious Goi Peace Award (Japan) in honor of his scientific contribution to world harmony and more recently in 2012 was chosen as Peace Ambassador for the "Thousand Peace Flags" project of the Argentinian Mil Milenios de Paz.

Hay House Titles of Related Interest

YOU CAN HEAL YOUR LIFE, the movie,
starring Louise Hay & Friends
(available as an online streaming video)
www.hayhouse.com/louise-movie

THE SHIFT, the movie,
starring Dr. Wayne W. Dyer
(available as an online streaming video)
www.hayhouse.com/the-shift-movie

♡

CHANGE YOUR THOUGHTS—CHANGE YOUR LIFE: Living the Wisdom of the Tao, by Dr. Wayne W. Dyer

DEEP TRUTH: Igniting the Memory of Our Origin, History, Destiny, and Fate, by Gregg Braden

LOVEABILITY: Knowing How to Love and Be Loved, by Robert Holden, Ph.D.

REWIRE YOUR BRAIN FOR LOVE: Creating Vibrant Relationships Using the Science of Mindfulness, by Marsha Lucas, Ph.D.

All of the above are available at your local bookstore or may be ordered by contacting Hay House (see next page).

♡ ♡ ♡

We hope you enjoyed this Hay House book. If you'd like to receive our online catalog featuring additional information on Hay House books and products, or if you'd like to find out more about the Hay Foundation, please contact:

Hay House LLC, P.O. Box 5100, Carlsbad, CA 92018-5100
(760) 431-7695 or (800) 654-5126
(760) 431-6948 (fax) or (800) 650-5115 (fax)
www.hayhouse.com® • www.hayfoundation.org

Published in Australia by: Hay House Australia Pty. Ltd.,
18/36 Ralph St., Alexandria NSW 2015
Phone: 612-9669-4299 • *Fax:* 612-9669-4144
www.hayhouse.com.au

Published in the United Kingdom by: Hay House UK, Ltd.,
The Sixth Floor, Watson House, 54 Baker Street, London W1U 7BU
Phone: +44 (0)20 3927 7290 • *Fax:* +44 (0)20 3927 7291
www.hayhouse.co.uk

Published in India by: Hay House Publishers India,
Muskaan Complex, Plot No. 3, B-2, Vasant Kunj, New Delhi 110 070
Phone: 91-11-4176-1620 • *Fax:* 91-11-4176-1630
www.hayhouse.co.in